A book for students, teachers, professionals, and community organizations

Dedicated to my parents, Ronald and Barbara Shea,
who spent their lives serving others

DESIGNING FOR SOCIAL CHANGE

Strategies for Community-Based Graphic Design

ANDREW SHEA

Foreword by **William Drenttel** Illustrations by **Ellen Lupton**

Princeton Architectural Press
New York

Design Briefs—essential texts on design.
Also available in this series:
D.I.Y. Design It Yourself, Ellen Lupton, 978-1-56898-552-7
Elements of Design, Gail Greet Hannah, 978-1-56898-329-5
Form + Code, Reas, McWilliams, and LUST, 978-1-56898-937-2
Geometry of Design, 2nd edition, Kimberly Elam, 978-1-61689-036-0
Graphic Design Theory, Helen Armstrong, 978-1-56898-772-9
Graphic Design Thinking, Ellen Lupton, 978-1-56898-979-2
Grid Systems, Kimberly Elam, 978-1-56898-465-0
Indie Publishing, Ellen Lupton, 978-1-56898-760-6
Lettering & Type, Bruce Willen, Nolen Strals, 978-1-56898-765-1
Participate, Helen Armstrong and Zvezdana Stojmirovic, 978-1-61689-025-4
Typographic Systems, Kimberly Elam, 978-1-56898-687-6
Thinking with Type, 2nd edition, Ellen Lupton, 978-1-56898-969-3
Visual Grammar, Christian Leborg, 978-1-56898-581-7
The Wayfinding Handbook, David Gibson, 978-1-56898-769-9

Design Briefs Series Editor
Ellen Lupton

Published by
Princeton Architectural Press
37 East Seventh Street
New York, New York 10003

For a free catalog of books, call 1.800.722.6657.
Visit our website at www.papress.com.

© 2012 Andrew Shea
All rights reserved
Printed and bound in China
15 14 13 12 4 3 2 1 First edition

No part of this book may be used or reproduced in any manner
without written permission from the publisher, except in the
context of reviews.

Every reasonable attempt has been made to identify owners
of copyright. Errors or omissions will be corrected in
subsequent editions.

Library of Congress Cataloging-in-Publication Data
Shea, Andrew, 1977–

Designing for social change : strategies for community-based
graphic design / Andrew Shea.
1st ed.
p. cm.
Includes bibliographical references.
ISBN 978-1-61689-047-6 (alk. paper)
1. Graphic arts—Social aspects. 2. Community arts projects.
I. Title. II. Title: Strategies for community-based graphic design.
NC997.S455 2012
741.6—dc23
                    2011039921

Editor
Nicola Bednarek Brower

Book and Cover Design
Andrew Shea

Typography
Gentium Plus, FF DIN

Photo Credits
Billy Delfs (16, 17, 19)
Installation re-created by Tyler Galloway (73)
Gini Woy (100, 104)
Craig Welsh (101, 103)
Toby Richards (102)

Table of Contents

Foreword

William Drenttel

In June 2008 I attended a workshop called "Design for Social Impact" sponsored by the Rockefeller Foundation at its center on Lake Como in Bellagio, Italy. In this unusually bucolic setting in the southern Alps, twenty designers from a dozen countries pondered the question of whether design could be an avenue for poverty alleviation, and how such efforts could be organized into effective and impactful initiatives by design practitioners, firms, and organizations. This meeting marked the beginning of a personal journey that changed both my life and my work.

In previous years, most of my friends and peers participated in what was commonly referred to as "nonprofit work." We might make our living producing branding for large companies, but we carved out a portion of our design practices to do "good work"—occasionally in our local communities, often for cultural organizations, and frequently with the sense that this was where our most creative opportunities lay. Such work was often done for no money or negligible fees: it was, quite literally, "nonprofit" work. Yet, this was the work that we entered in competitions, retained for our portfolios, and displayed proudly at conferences, forming the basis for many a creative reputation. It was graphic design doing good; Robin Hood stealing from the rich to help the poor; even a form of tithing, a ritualized percentage of our practice given back to God.

This approach to nonprofit design, whether engaged with ballet companies, local food banks, or voter registration initiatives, had another, darker side. It was often about the work we could showcase, not the people we were helping. It was often amateurish—designers making forays into education or health care with little practical knowledge or meaningful experience. It privileged the teacher, not the student; the client, not the user; the provider, not the person in need. It was too often design about design, design for the sake of design, designers preaching to one another about design's capability to create impact.

At that Bellagio workshop I realized that design for social change could mean something very different. The participants talked about working with social enterprises, NGOs, foundations, corporations, and governments. We argued the vocabulary of social innovation, collaborative systems, and systemic change. We envisioned designing methods for poverty alleviation, social justice, and sustainable environments. And at every turn there were nagging questions, challenges without obvious answers. How do we capture innovations and replicate them? How do we move from effective programs to sustainable systems? Can we collaborate across the spectrum of design methodologies and genres to generate deeper, larger, longer-lasting solutions? How could such collaborations be organized, funded, and implemented? How could we measure our effectiveness, learn from our failures, and implement metrics for gauging sustained impact? How can we create programs and solutions of a scale commensurate with the scale of the actual problems confronting us?

I have since come to believe that social design defines a new kind of designer. It needs to be expansively conceived beyond trained designers to include end users and social participants. Social design cannot be a subspecialty of the design profession (like graphic design, package design, product design, service design, and so on), but is a larger activity that depends upon design in all its forms—thought, processes, tools, methodologies, skills, histories, systems—to contribute to the needs of a larger society. It implies at once an attitude and an approach to life: as such, it can help us frame how we want to live in the future. It is therefore inherently pragmatic and results-oriented, simultaneously humble and ambitious, and fundamentally optimistic and forward-looking.

So where do we start?

Designing for Social Change is one place to begin. It's a toolkit of strategies, case studies, and stories, offering new opportunities for approaching social design in our communities. It presents students and schools as active participants, designers and design firms as social innovators, and communities as both rich laboratories for experimentation and receptive locations for creative approaches and new ideas. It includes successes and failures, and, with thoughtful reading, offers both evidence and learning that can inform future social design work and projects. Importantly, it suggests that collaboration between designers, and across schools and communities, has the potential to generate even more compelling future initiatives—and the potential for deeper design engagements that successfully impact the quality of life in our towns and cities. *Designing for Social Change* should be the guidebook of a youthful, nascent movement, one that is changing the definition and the role of design. As a designer, this is an exciting place to start.

Preface

Graphic design has often been associated with glossy magazines, elaborate advertising campaigns, or fancy book covers, but many designers today use their skills for a very different kind of design work. Known as "design for social impact," "human-centered design," or "design for social change," the field of social design attracts increasingly more graphic designers who crave a chance to work with underserved clients as an alternative to the more traditional design jobs in large corporations and advertising firms. They want to work closely with communities that need their help most and actively participate in combating complex social problems.

I first worked on a community-based project as Professor Bernard Canniffe's teaching assistant for a class at Maryland Institute College of Art (MICA) called "Design Coalition," where graphic design students get paired up with largely underserved and underfunded communities.[1] My role was to lead six undergraduate students in a collaboration with NF-MidAtlantic, a nonprofit organization that supports people who have a largely unknown disease called "neurofibromatosis" (NF). This genetic disorder of the nervous system causes tumors to form on the nerves inside and outside the body. People suffering from it often feel socially isolated because of the disfiguring nature of these tumors.

We started the project by interviewing patients, their caretakers, and parents of children who suffer from NF. We soon became overwhelmed by their complex personal stories and by what we learned about the disease. NF affects all races, all ethnic groups, and both sexes equally, and it usually gets worse with age. Fifty percent of the people who suffer from the disease can pass it on to their children, although it can also be caused spontaneously by a genetic mutation. There is no cure for NF, and the tumors can become cancerous.[2] NF-MidAtlantic needed help to raise awareness and to promote the organization, but we wondered what we as graphic designers could do to help people who suffer from this incurable physical disorder.

As a group, we realized that this was more than just another design job. We hoped that our efforts would make the public more accepting of NF patients and believed that we could help empower the NF community. During the semester, small groups of students worked on various initiatives meant to raise awareness, to help people cope with the disease, and to strengthen the organization, including an interactive web page, beanbag toys, a sixteen-page tabloid newspaper, and a new logo. As the project leader, I had the responsibility of guiding the students through the process of working with the organization. We spent a lot of time talking to various community members but seldom met with the decision makers at NF-MidAtlantic to tell them about our progress and to consult with them about our ideas. At the end of the semester, NF-MidAtlantic rejected our proposals.

I was left wondering what we should have done differently, how we should have worked together with the organization to produce a positive outcome. The project had convinced me that I should spend more time using my design skills to support civic and cultural causes, but I realized that there were significant gaps in my knowledge and experience. I started to read everything I could find about social and community-based design projects, scouring the library for books and journal articles that might be helpful and searching the internet in hopes that I would find databases stuffed with wisdom from other graphic designers. But while I found plenty of inspiring awareness and advocacy projects, I rarely came across the kind of detailed background information that I was hoping for.

Most websites by graphic designers and design studios involved with social design included a page or paragraph about their process, which usually involved some variation of research, analysis, prototyping, and production. Among these, two resources were especially useful: IDEO's Human-Centered Design Toolkit[3] and the firm's Design for Social Impact: A How-To Guide.[4] IDEO created the Human-Centered Design Toolkit for companies and organizations that conduct ethnographic research, whereas its how-to guide provides an overview of the nuances of working with a community. These two documents—both funded by the Rockefeller Foundation—provided me with a lot of what I was looking for, though I got lost in their wealth of details. Emily Pilloton, product designer and founder of the nonprofit Project H Design, prepared a similar resource with her Design Revolution Toolkit, a short document that "provides values and tactics for how each of us—design practitioners, students, and educators—can design better solutions for the greater good: for people instead of clients, for change instead of consumption."[5] Pilloton's toolkit made me wonder how these "tactics" might influence the process of actual projects—

especially those undertaken by graphic designers—and first gave me the idea of writing this book.

In all of these documents I read a lot about the importance of designing "with not for" the community, but I was still unsure of what "design with" really means in the course of a graphic design project. I knew that we needed to work with NF-MidAtlantic, but I did not know how. I came to believe that a solid understanding of how to successfully connect with a community—a list of community engagement strategies—would have helped us frame the design challenge, spot problems before they became irreversible, and guided our work. This topic is not new. Academics, activists, business consultants, educators, and social workers make up a portion of the people from various disciplines who have studied this subject for decades. I often looked to their insights when writing this book and cited their research throughout.

I learned that community engagement is as complex as humans themselves. It requires designers to work with a range of people who have strong opinions and a lot of emotions and pride invested in their community. A single logo or poster design rarely addresses the totality of the social issue that prompted the designer's engagement in the first place. Instead, designers need to find ways to get to the root of the problem, which is often part of a larger, messier system of issues that need to be dealt with.

It may be unrealistic to set specific goals at the outset of community-based projects, but there are a handful of nonmonetary results that designers might aim to achieve: helping community members establish a common vision and strengthening their interest to work together toward that vision; clarifying complex information or data with graphics that increase the community's knowledge and competence; improving the way an organization communicates with community members; helping community members improve their quality of life by raising awareness around safety, health, and environmental issues in a way that empowers them to take responsibility;[6] increasing the efficiency of a process; and improving the community's social and human capital with better social ties, networks, and support.[7]

The process of helping communities in need often motivates designers to work on similar projects in the future. William Drenttel, of Winterhouse Institute and Design Observer, talked about the power of this continual transformation at the A Better World by Design Conference in the fall of 2009, emphasizing the strength of alumni networks that steadily grow in size and expertise. Drenttel's most impressive example was Teach for America, which in 2009 had trained twenty-five thousand volunteers to teach in underserved schools. The experience of working for Teach for America inspires most of its participants to continue serving others. In fact, 63 percent of these volunteers still teach, and many also make an impact by sitting on educational boards. The value of organizations like this grows long into the future.[8] A similar ripple effect in the design community could place graphic designers in key positions across industries where they could make a positive impact. This book provides designers with a detailed guide to help in that process.

The twenty case studies that follow contain many insights about working with communities. While similarities exist regarding the types of problems designers run into and how they engage communities, I divided the case studies into groups that illustrate ten important community engagement strategies that can help you work through your own social design project. Use them to frame a design challenge, guide your process, and identify and solve problems.

Acknowledgments

Before *Designing for Social Change* became a book, it was my Master of Fine Arts thesis project at MICA. While aspects of it changed since I started the project, my collaboration with graphic design educators, students, and practitioners remained a central focus. This book would not exist without their willingness to talk about their work with community groups, reflect on what they learned from the process, and help me pinpoint strategies that might help other designers. Many people supported me along the way. Bernard Canniffe allowed me to lead my first community-based design project, encouraged me to become invested in the lives of the NF community, and convinced me that we designers need to talk about the effectiveness of our efforts. I collaborated with Mark Alcasabas and Virginia Sasser, who were also part of Canniffe's class, to compile the first version of the community engagement strategies in this book. Jennifer Cole Phillips challenged me with important questions during the formative phase of my research, and David Barringer showed me how to scrutinize my writing as much as my visual design work. Ellen Lupton encouraged me to write about design and to turn my thesis into a book. She shared her wisdom about the publishing process, she edited my writing with lightning speed and with insights that were always relevant and often provocative, and she became a trusted sounding board. I am deeply grateful for everyone at Princeton Architectural Press who helped me build this book, especially Jennifer Lippert, Kevin Lippert, and my editor, Nicola Bednarek Brower. Finally, my wife, Kristin, has been a patient listener and steadfast supporter who granted me the time to research and write this book.

Immerse Yourself

In its broadest sense the term *community* refers to a group of people who share something, such as a place, culture, emotions, or occupation.[1] While their commonality may be their greatest strength, the wide range of perceptions, interests, enterprises, and ways of interacting among community members is often the biggest obstacle for graphic designers who want to help.[2] In order to accurately understand a community's needs, it is extremely important to gain a thorough knowledge of the community and experience firsthand the lives and environment of community members.

Immersion refers to any number of ways you may spend time with the community. For example, designers can immerse themselves by taking tours through a neighborhood, regularly visiting community leaders, conducting focus groups,[3] and canvassing the community. Sometimes you may need to fade into the background and observe, while at other times you might need to work side by side with members of the community.

Consider community and organizational members as partners in all aspects of the design process. These partnerships are the currency of community engagement,[4] and projects can suffer if these relationships are not nourished. Immersion often opens up new opportunities that can lead to new discoveries, but designers need to be prepared to give up a certain amount of control and let the community's input inform their design decisions in order to mobilize the community's assets, strengths, and resources.[5]

Clear communication by the project leader is a key part of the immersive process and the project as a whole. The leader plays different roles, such as motivator, champion of the cause, planner, relationship builder, facilitator, and conflict handler.[6] He or she defines and tracks responsibilities of team members to prevent duplication and to ensure that the results are efficiently delivered.[7] The leader also helps the group understand and define the design challenges of the project, while identifying what questions need to be asked along the way—something that cannot be achieved without an intimate vantage point.

While nearly every case study in this book involved a process that started with immersion, the following two projects by the Canary Project and MICA's Center for Design Practice show how different levels of getting to know a community can lead to different results.

CareS Mobile Safety Center

Redesigning a mobile health bus to reach a bilingual audience

The CareS Mobile Safety Center parks outside schools, medical clinics, health fairs, and other venues in Baltimore. The colorfully painted, forty-foot vehicle has a retrofitted interior that looks like a normal home but educates visitors about safety hazards. Teaching parents how to prevent burns, poisoning, falls, strangulation, and other injuries in the home, it meets an important need in Baltimore City, where childhood death due to fire reached four times the national average between 2002 and 2004.[1]

The Johns Hopkins Center for Injury Research & Policy created this interactive house on wheels in 2004. Since then it attracted over eighteen thousand visitors through 2009,[2] 96 percent of whom reported learning something new during their tour.[3] Yet its organizers found that the vehicle needed to communicate more effectively to Baltimore's growing Hispanic communities, so they approached MICA's Center for Design Practice (CDP) to modify the existing design of the van in a way that would reach both English- and Spanish-speaking audiences.

The CDP occupies the top floor of a row house on the MICA campus. Here Mike Weikert, founder and director of this multidisciplinary design studio, prepares students for design

bringing child safety to our community

PROJECT DETAILS

DESIGNS Poster, brochure, exhibition; typeface: Museo Sans
DATE September to December 2009
LOCATION Baltimore, Maryland
LEADERS Mike Weikert and Ryan Clifford (Center for Design Practice, MICA)
DESIGNERS Five graphic design students (Center for Design Practice, MICA)
PARTNERS Stephanie Parsons, Eileen McDonald, Andrea Gielen, and Kira McGroarty
(Johns Hopkins Center for Injury Research & Policy)
WEBSITE www.micasocialdesign.com/cares-mobile-safety-center

Previous page
The CareS Mobile Safety Center is a converted recreation vehicle that travels to neighborhoods and educates communities about home safety.

Below
Stephanie Parsons demonstrates home safety in the kitchen.

leadership by partnering with outside organizations "to translate ideas and information into tangible outcomes with the potential to change behaviors and make a positive impact on society."[4] The CDP has been part of various initiatives since its inception in 2007. Some of its projects have promoted arts education and better nutrition, consuming less energy, and raising awareness about lead poisoning and food deserts in Baltimore City. Working on the CareS vehicle was a natural fit for the center, whose process includes engaging partners who have similar values; getting together the right team of people; discovering the essence of the problem through immersion; and transforming complex information for those who need it most.[5]

The five graphic design students who were chosen to work on this project started by learning more about CareS from their partners at Johns Hopkins University: Stephanie Parsons, Eileen McDonald, Andrea Gielen, and Kira McGroarty. "CareS stands for Children Are Safe," Gielen explained in an interview with the *JHU Gazette.* "Every year more than one thousand Baltimore children are hospitalized as a result of an injury—that's almost three children every day who do not need to be suffering from these preventable injuries."[6] The student's research continued in Baltimore's Latino neighborhoods, where they learned how safety is advertised to bilingual audiences. They also took an informal tour of the CareS vehicle. Led by Parsons, the forty-five-minute tour points out hazards in the home, such as a pan handle extending out from the kitchen stove, toys littering the staircase, and an upright toilet seat in the bathroom, and explains how to prevent injuries. The tour ends in the vehicle's bedroom, which fills up with smoke to simulate a fire. Bright graphics help visitors remember what they learned.

After this initial research phase the students brainstormed ways to improve and broaden the vehicle's messages. They designed

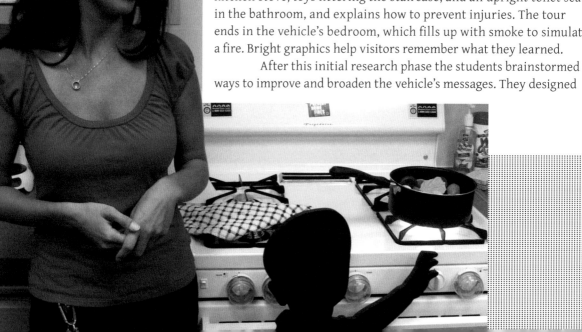

LEARN ABOUT SAFETY IN YOUR HOME

CaReS Safety Center
Fun, Free Exhibits
Low Cost Safety Products

APRENDEN ACERCA DE SEGURIDAD EN SU HOGAR

CaReS Centro de Seguridad
Exhibiciones Divertidos y Gratis
Productos Economicos de Seguridad

Above
Bilingual signs to be placed outside the CaReS
vehicle as an invitation into the truck

graphical prototypes depicting home safety scenarios and showed them to focus groups made up of both English- and Spanish-speaking parents, who shared their own home safety practices. The participants emphasized the need for interactive education and the use of pictures and diagrams in educational materials. Some also reported that they would be hesitant to visit the CaReS center because they could not tell what type of services were being offered from the graphics on the vehicle.

The students reconvened with their partners from Johns Hopkins University and decided to create new materials and products that were personal, speaking directly to the visitor; participatory, giving the visitor an enhanced role; physical, reducing the need for written language; and universal, speaking to everyone regardless of literacy or language spoken. Their designs included a poster in both Spanish and English that invites hesitant onlookers inside the vehicle as well as a brochure that visitors can take home.

While the interior of the safety center did not change, the students designed a set of universal graphics (a green check mark and a red exclamation mark) to increase participation and improve the tour through the vehicle. Visitors now have to guess which exhibits are safety hazards and which are safety precautions. Correct guesses result in Parsons attaching the green check mark to the exhibit, while she puts the red sign on when visitors guess incorrectly and proceeds to explain the hazard. Not only does this system communicate more effectively to bilingual visitors, but it also creates a more engaging tour. "One of the major things we learned from the design students is the power of simplicity," Parsons says. "As health educators, I think we have an urge to give all the information that we have available, but, as we learned through focus groups and from the students, less is more."

DESIGN CHALLENGE
Modifying existing designs to communicate with Baltimore's growing Hispanic communities more effectively.

ENGAGEMENT STRATEGY
Immersing into the community by touring the CaReS vehicle, visiting Baltimore's Hispanic neighborhoods, and conducting focus groups.

DESIGN STRATEGY
Creating interactive, heavily illustrated designs that reduce the need for written language.

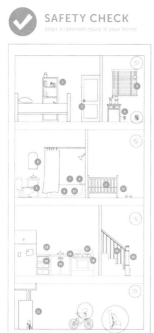

The new designs are personal, participatory, physical, and universal, speaking to everyone regardless of literacy or language spoken.

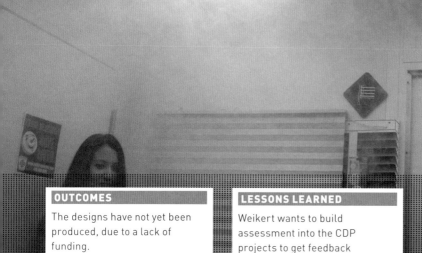

OUTCOMES

The designs have not yet been produced, due to a lack of funding.

LESSONS LEARNED

Weikert wants to build assessment into the CDP projects to get feedback about the effectiveness of his students' designs.

The green and red icon system was also used on the take-home handout. Each side of this illustrated brochure shows a four-story home with home safety reminders that are highlighted by the colored icons and described in both English and Spanish. In addition, the students created a series of triptychs that depict possible hazards (such as an upright toilet seat), how a child might be injured by the hazard (drowning), and how to prevent the hazard (close and latch the toilet seat).

Weikert was happy with the design outcomes. "The biggest challenge is time," he says, "but we did a really thorough job for the time and scope of the sixteen-week project." The students' efforts to immerse into the community by becoming familiar with the CARES center, researching Latino neighborhoods, and conducting focus groups with bilingual parents paid off with informed designs that collectively addressed how to talk about home safety. The designs will certainly reach a larger audience, but Weikert admits, "It would be useful to be involved in the assessment of the tools we created…to see if our process and solutions yield tangible results." The CARES team is currently waiting for more funds to produce CDP's designs, but "Once those funds arrive, the designs will be produced and evaluated," Parsons promises.

Opposite, bottom
The CARES Mobile tour ends with a fire simulation.

Opposite, top
A one-page checklist that outlines home safety room by room

Below
Three spreads of the bilingual home safety brochure

SAFETY CHECK
CHEQUE DE SEGURIDAD

Injury Prevention in the Home
La Prevención de Lesiones en el Hogar

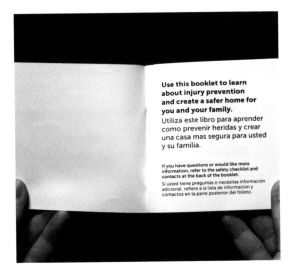

Use this booklet to learn about injury prevention and create a safer home for you and your family.
Utiliza este libro para aprender como prevenir heridas y crear una casa mas segura para usted y su familia.

If you have questions or would like more information, refer to the safety checklist and contacts at the back of the booklet.
Si usted tiene preguntas o necesitas información adicional, refiere a la lista de información y contactos en la parte posterior del folleto.

Green Patriot Posters

Designing an ad campaign against global warming

Global warming is a divisive issue. It affects us all but building a consensus to do something about it has not been easy. Edward Morris, cofounder and director (with Susannah Sayler) of the Canary Project, wanted to address this problem by creating a national campaign that focuses on "producing visual media, events, and artwork that build public understanding of human-induced climate change and energize commitment to solutions."[1] The Canary Project spreads its message by documenting environmental changes, creating public art and installations, and producing educational exhibitions and presentations.

In 2008 Morris teamed up with fellow designer Dmitri Siegel and chose Cleveland as the site of an ad campaign to find out whether graphic design can unify people around the issue of climate change. Global warming does not catch headlines in this city, which has seen its industries move away and its population shrink from 900,000 to 450,000 since 1950. Thirty percent of its residents live in poverty. Nevertheless, as Morris puts it, "The heart of the country is the key to positive movement on this issue. Cities such as Cleveland have the most to gain from reconfiguring the manufacturing sector."

THIS BUS IS AN

SAULT VEHICLE

HE FIGHT AGAINST GLOBAL WARMING.

BE A

GREEN PATRIOT.

GREEN PATRIOT POSTERS.ORG

PROJECT DETAILS

DESIGNS Advertisements for eighty buses; typeface: Agenda

DATE July to September 2008

LOCATION Cleveland, Ohio

LEADERS Edward Morris and Susannah Sayler (the Canary Project), Dmitri Siegel

DESIGNERS Michael Bierut and Kai Salmela (Pentagram)

PARTNERS City of Cleveland Office of Sustainability, Green City Blue Lake

WEBSITE www.greenpatriotposters.org/bierut.php

An important partner on the ground in Cleveland became Green City Blue Lake, an institute that educates the public about living sustainably in the twenty-first century. Together, the two organizations identified aspects of the movement that would resonate with Cleveland residents. Their primary goal was to generate pride in the city's revitalization efforts that are centered on green jobs and better public transportation and to inspire people to think and talk about environmental issues. The resulting campaign, called Green Patriot Posters, aligns sustainability with personal values across the political spectrum. The theme of patriotism was chosen to promote pride of place, to transcend prejudices, and to increase the feeling of personal investment in the issue.

After determining the primary objectives of the posters, the Canary Project hired Michael Bierut and his team at Pentagram to design the campaign. Bierut's goal was to fit the posters in with other advertisements used on public transportation and for the designs to be easily understood by the broad range of people who ride Cleveland's buses. The ads therefore do not use tricky layouts, ambiguous imagery, or arcane fonts. Instead, Bierut used simple, text-based messages that are set in the Agenda typeface because, as he says, "It has a little bit of that 1930s propaganda feel."

Previous page
The exterior bus ads were applied to about eighty buses.

Left and opposite
Bierut appropriated and modified the classic silhouette of a Revolutionary War soldier as a way to build broad support against global warming.

OH O IS GREEN PATRIOT COUNTRY.
GREEN PATRIOT POSTERS.ORG

The theme of patriotism was chosen to promote pride of place, to transcend prejudices, and to increase the feeling of personal investment in the issue.

Three ads, which were placed on both the inside and the outside of the city's buses, made up the campaign. Each used the silhouette of a Revolutionary War soldier set in green, combined with slogans that promote the patriotism of using mass transit. The slogan on the outside of the buses, "This Bus Is an Assault Vehicle in the Fight against Global Warming," was inspired by Woody Guthrie's inscription on his guitar, "This machine kills fascists." As Bierut puts it, "I love the way that [Guthrie's] statement repositions the supposedly gentle, nonthreatening world of acoustic folk music as something to be feared. Our line attempts to transform a message that could be dismissed as irrelevant do-goodism into something brawny and positive. We tried to make the overall graphic tone feel similarly straightforward and powerful." The ads were funded by the George Gund Foundation and EarthKeepers powered by Changents, and were displayed on about eighty buses.

Morris's original funding proposal to the George Gund Foundation called for an extensive research period that involved recruiting and educating teenagers to conduct surveys to find out which sustainability themes resonated with the people in their neighborhoods. He also wanted to hire marketing students at Case

DESIGN CHALLENGE

Positioning global warming as a patriotic issue that can revitalize Cleveland's economy and improve public transportation.

ENGAGEMENT STRATEGY

Building partnerships with Cleveland's Office of Sustainability and Green City Blue Lake to help frame the topic in a way that resonates with Cleveland's citizens.

DESIGN STRATEGY

Using simple, text-based messages combined with straightforward graphics.

OUTCOMES

Around eighty buses displayed
the advertisements and twenty
volunteers rode the buses for
a day to talk with people about
global warming and to gauge the
effectiveness of the ads.

LESSONS LEARNED

Spending more time immersed
in the local communities might
have helped the group make the
ads more relevant for Cleveland
citizens. In hindsight Morris thinks
he should have spent more money
on outreach and less on the ad
space rented.

Western Reserve University to conduct follow-up surveys that would assess the impact on communities. Ultimately, only the production and display of the bus ads received financial backing. Morris was essentially an outsider to the city, when he first started to work on Green Patriot Posters, which may explain why the funders did not believe in the full potential of the project.

The designer did manage to find twenty volunteers to ride the buses for a day and use the ads as a prompt to talk to people about mass transit, the future of Cleveland, and the role that sustainability might play in the city's development. They learned that those people who paid attention to bus ads had trouble figuring out what they were about and did not really care about climate change or sustainability. Nor did they believe in the possibility of green jobs.

When asked what he would change if he could do the project again, Morris responded that he would reverse the priorities of the campaign, spending more money on the outreach and less on the number of buses he rented ad space on. He believes that the project would have been more successful if his team had spent time immersed in the local communities, where they may have learned how to make the ads more relevant to Cleveland citizens by connecting them to other civic events. Instead of creating a sense of pride and solidarity around his campaign from within Cleveland, Morris tried to orchestrate it from a distance.

While the campaign may not have affected the people who encountered the posters in Cleveland, it has since expanded to Dorchester, Massachusetts, and exists as an ongoing project. The designs have also been well received in the press. Green Patriot Posters was cited by the *Cleveland Plain Dealer* as one of the best public art projects in Cleveland in 2008, and the designs were recently selected for the 2011 Cooper-Hewitt National Design Triennial exhibition, Why Design Now? However, Morris acknowledges that gaining accolades in the design world says nothing about what actually works to invigorate a specific community.

Opposite
Twenty volunteers rode the buses and talked to pedestrians for a day, using the ads as prompts to talk about mass transit and how sustainability initiatives can help the city's development.

Below
One of two banners that Bierut designed for exterior bus panels

CREATING MORE THAN
THREE MILLION
NEW JOBS

BE A
GREEN PATRIOT.
GREEN PATRIOT POSTERS.ORG

Build Trust

Build strong relationships with the communities you work with to learn how you can best help them. An underserved or exploited community will be skeptical of the efforts of outsiders. They may have seen other volunteers come into their neighborhoods and try to make an impact in a short period of time without success. A few conversations with community leaders will rarely win over a community and might undermine the entire initiative, preventing any substantive social change.

Prevention By Design, a community planning organization based in Berkeley, California, points out "There is no holy grail for community involvement. It requires full authenticity and relationship. Anything less, and people go away feeling used."[1]

Think about your efforts as part of cultivating personal relationships and design partnerships in order to achieve another important engagement goal: winning the community's trust.[2] Help community members in their daily operations, make a meal for them, or quickly meet one of their basic design needs. Show them that you are serious about partnering with them to improve their lives.

Earning the trust of the community will help you connect emotionally with community members and their problems, and will help you take pride in your design solution. IDEO's engagement tool Design for Social Impact highlights the importance of building empathy and refers to "empathy field trips" as a central part of community engagement for people who have little or no knowledge of that community.[3] In a sense you may need to play the role of an anthropologist to gain an understanding of a community's problem. As you build trust and understand a community's needs, you will become an invested partner and your designs will reflect the personality and ethos of community members.

Approach each situation with an open mind and assume that your opinions will change as you work. As you build friendships with community members, their experiences should guide your research toward an effective design solution. The following two projects show designers working toward cultivating these trust relationships with very different communities: young boxers at an inner-city gym and students at elementary schools.

No Hooks before Books

Promoting a boxing and
educational program

Graphic design graduate students Mark Alcasabas and Virginia
Sasser found out about UMAR Boxing from a wrinkled flyer
that had been photocopied hundreds of times. Like many flyers
that clutter community boards and street poles, it was barely
legible, but the title piqued their interest: "No Hooks before
Books." Alcasabas and Sasser were part of the Design Coalition,
a class at MICA where graphic design students work with largely
underserved and underfunded communities. Canniffe, their
professor and then cochair of the graphic design department, had
visited UMAR a few semesters before and gave his students a copy
of the flyer, encouraging them to contact the organization.

UMAR Boxing is a nonprofit after-school program that
provides boxing training for children who participate in academic
tutoring. Marvin McDowell founded the organization in 1999 to
spread his message that combining education and athletic training
can get children off the street. He chose the uplifting Arabic name
UMAR (which means "flourishing; to live, to prosper") to help the
gym stand out as a source of hope in West Baltimore, where street
pressures breed drug dealers and gang problems. McDowell's goal

PROJECT DETAILS

DESIGNS Thirty-two-page newsprint tabloid, flyer redesign, DVD design; typeface: Knockout
DATE January to May 2009
LOCATION West Baltimore, Maryland
LEADERS Mark Alcasabas, Virginia Sasser, and Bernard Canniffe (Design Coalition, MICA)
DESIGNERS Mark Alcasabas and Virginia Sasser
PARTNERS UMAR Boxing

Previous page
The designers created a tabloid to promote UMAR's program.

Left
Some of the boxers at UMAR Boxing have gone on to win title matches in their division.

Below
One of the last spreads in the tabloid itemizes the cost of boxing gear.

Opposite, top
Original flyer

Opposite, bottom
Redesigned flyer

THE PRICE OF BOXING GEAR
$70 TRAINING HEADGEAR
$40 SPEEDBAG
$45 SUPER BAG GLOVES
$60 SAFETY TRAINING GLOVES
$45 NO-FOUL PROTECTOR
$50 PUNCH MITT
$60 COMPETITION HEADGEAR
$160 100 LB HEAVY BAG
$95 SPARMATE TIMER
$10 JUMP ROPE

"Boxing is one sport
that will humble the
toughest kid."

Marvin McDowell

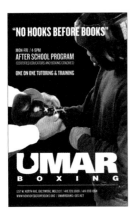

is to promote UMAR's unique educational component to other youth boxing programs throughout the mid-Atlantic region, and Alcasabas and Sasser offered to help advance the nonprofit's innovative approach and attract donors by designing promotional materials. The students initially focused on developing a relationship with the community, spending the first two of the four months they worked on the project gathering information about the program and meeting the teachers and boxers. They concentrated on building trust with community members, because many well-intentioned volunteers had broken their promises to these children and boxers in the past.

The gym used by UMAR has a rich and diverse visual culture. The strong graphics of the gritty space include screenprinted posters of boxing matches and motivational slogans, such as "Put the Guns down, Put the Gloves up," some of which are handwritten on fading paper or printed on fabric. The colorful posters match the energy of the gym, which floods with children every day after school. A sense of family can be felt throughout the space, as boxers train with each other.

Alcasabas and Sasser's first step was a quick redesign of the flyer that had introduced them to UMAR and which circulates throughout West Baltimore. The new design replaced the crooked typography and grainy illustrations with a large photograph of a boxer and details that specified the what, when, how, and where of the program. The bold photograph increased the visibility of the flyer, which remained black and white to make it easily reproducible. The new flyer helped the designers prove that they respected the integrity of the UMAR community and that they were sincere about offering real solutions. The children started to bond with Sasser about boxing and school, while the older boxers invited Alcasabas to matches. Trainers and teachers opened up to both of them, and McDowell, impressed with the flyer, was open to suggestions for future designs.

DESIGN CHALLENGE

Helping a boxing gym promote their unique boxing/educational program as a way to get children off the street.

ENGAGEMENT STRATEGY

Building trust with the community by regularly visiting the gym, documenting the activities there, and getting to know the boxers, trainers, and children.

DESIGN STRATEGY

Using the gym's visual culture and the aesthetics of the West Baltimore neighborhoods as an inspiration.

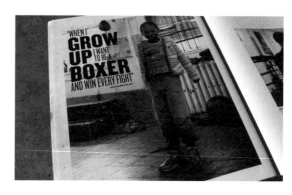

"To be a good boxer,
you have to be
a good thinker."

Marvin McDowell

OUTCOMES

Two thousand copies of the tabloid were printed and are being used by UMAR Boxing to spread its message and attract donors.

LESSONS LEARNED

The students learned that it pays off to build strong relationships with community members. This gave them an intimate vantage point, which helped them come to a successful design solution.

Alcasabas and Sasser became personally invested in the project as they spent more time at UMAR. Their design decisions were based on these experiences, which gave them an intimate vantage point to assess, understand, and help the West Baltimore community. They wanted to promote the organization, but they also wanted their design to speak to the boxing world. Taking inspiration from the visuals of the gym and the neighborhoods of West Baltimore, they decided to create a black-and-white tabloid that McDowell could show off at boxing matches, hand out to potential donors, and use to encourage young children to join the gym.

The thirty-two-page tabloid features original writing by the designers that depicts UMAR as a source of hope and dispels the popular belief that boxing is an unsafe sport reserved for dense brutes. The designers wanted "to capture the essence of a gym that smells like sweat," as they describe it. Bold black-and-white photographs convey the gym's personality, and the text is set in Knockout, designed by Jonathan Hoefler, to recall the traditional look of boxing posters. The tabloid, aptly titled "No Hooks before Books," demonstrates the importance of UMAR Boxing as a tutoring center and a boxing gym, as well as its very real need for funding. When Alcasabas and Sasser delivered the two thousand printed tabloids, the children were enthusiastic, crowding around the students, trying to find themselves in the images, and pointing out what they liked.

Reflecting back on the project, Alcasabas points out his frustrations with the semester schedule: "I wish we had more time to spend at UMAR and at boxing matches. The project might have gone more smoothly if we had longer to learn from people at the gym instead of thinking about our deadline and our final product." Canniffe empathizes with Alcasabas's comments: "I struggle with what success means and how these types of projects exist in academic structures that can be restrictive and punitive. One thing I have found to be true is once students take part in these projects and these classes, they find it difficult to accept and participate in theoretical studio classes, as they feel they are irrelevant. This conflict is common to all institutions. Success is taking students outside the institutional bubble and into the community." Canniffe proposes that design schools educate their students to be less of a "service provider, and to explore and celebrate the idea of designer as social listener and responder."

Opposite, top
The designers spent a lot of time with students and boxers, whose quotes are peppered throughout the tabloid.

Opposite, bottom left
This page in the tabloid lists boxing instruction and tutoring costs that are funded by donations.

Opposite, bottom right
Children of all ages come to the UMAR gym.

A Book by Its Cover: Reading Stereotypes

Fostering contact between children of different ethnicities to prevent stereotypes from forming

Many Americans have a skewed view of Arabic culture. News coverage fueled by fear and controversy, coupled with widespread misunderstandings of Islam, has led to unfair vilification of a largely peaceful, accepting, and pious culture. Graphic design student Ramzy Masri, born to a Caucasian mother and a Saudi-Arabian father, experienced this intolerance firsthand, especially after 9/11. He also vividly recalls his father's stories of people throwing garbage and full cans of soda at him from moving vehicles when he moved to America in the 1980s. "I never understood why such a beautiful culture is associated with so much negativity," Masri says. As someone who knows the perspectives of both ethnicities, he felt emboldened to use his graphic design skills as a mediator between the two cultures. Looking for funding for his plan, he applied for Worldstudio's Design Ignites Change contest, which challenges students to use design thinking as a means of making a positive change in their communities. Masri's project, A Book by Its Cover, was one of three proposals that won an Implementation Award, providing grant money to make the project a reality.

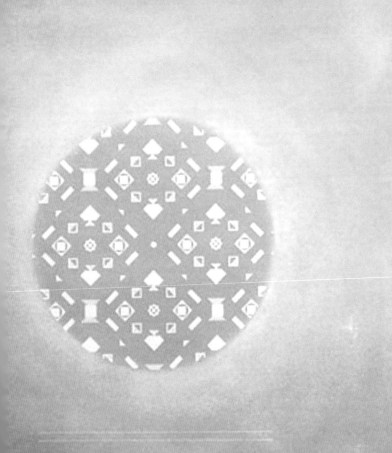

Itadel

tima

PROJECT DETAILS

DESIGNS Surveys, series of children's books
DATE 2009 to 2010
LOCATION Kansas City, Missouri
LEADER Ramzy Masri
DESIGNER Ramzy Masri
PARTNERS Kansas City Art Institute, Islamic School of Greater Kansas City, Garfield Elementary, Design Ignites Change
WEBSITE www.designigniteschange.org/projects/103-a-book-by-its-cover-reading-stereotypes

To get a better idea of what he was up against, Masri started by identifying and researching how stereotypes form. As sociologist Charles E. Hurst states, "One reason for stereotypes is the lack of personal concrete familiarity that individuals have with persons in other racial or ethnic groups. Lack of familiarity encourages the lumping together of unknown individuals."[1] Masri polled fellow students and teachers at random to amass a visual landscape of existing stereotypes and to find their common thread. Asking people to draw a map of the Middle East and a picture of an Arabic person, Masri was shocked by some of the responses: "I received maps that looked more like an imaginary world than the Middle East. I also got back images of turbans, bombs, machine guns, and AK-47s." If nothing else, these experiments convinced the designer that stereotypes about Arabs were more widespread than he had initially thought.

His research, which included conversations with educators in Kansas City, led Masri to believe that the only real way to prevent discrimination is to work with children between the ages of eight and ten years old, before they develop fully formed racial identities and while they are still open about the way they identify with others. He decided to create a set of children's books that deal with a variety of issues that contribute to discrimination and intolerance. Each book's plot is centered around a protagonist who struggles with difference in one way or another. In one book a circle and square want to marry, despite their parents' geometric bigotry. Another title tells the story of a triangle who realizes that he is the only triangle at school, and yet another is about a lonely circle who makes a friend. All of the characters have Arabic names and face many of the same problems Arabic immigrants have to deal with.

Previous page
Masri created a series of books to teach tolerance to children.

Below
About two hundred children participated in Masri's program.

Opposite, top
A student's drawing of the Middle East

Opposite, bottom
Masri reads to a classroom.

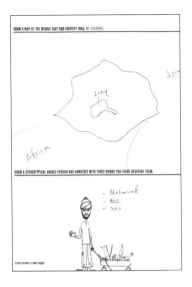

Masri was studying constructivism and the Bauhaus while he worked on A Book by Its Cover, which largely influenced his design solution. "I looked to El Lissitzky's *About 2 Squares* as a case study that illustrated how complicated problems could be articulated in simple and poetic ways. The universal implications of raw geometry had many interesting parallels to ideas of racial identity. Using geometric forms as characters, Lissitzky allows his audience to use their imagination to complete the story. His shapes are metaphors, not articulations of exact forms. By appropriating this strategy, I could draw an Arabic person without actually drawing an Arabic person. What lesson was I hoping the kids would learn from my books? That we're really more alike than different."

This strategy was fitting for another reason: Islam does not allow the use of iconography, nor can Mohammed be depicted, like Christians depict Jesus. As a result, a rich tradition of geometric patterning has emerged in Islamic art and architecture. While Masri chose abstraction in the design of the books as an appropriate way of approaching this complex issue, he allowed his and his family's story to heavily influence the narratives. "I looked to my father every step of the way to ensure that my decisions reflected Islamic beliefs and the Arabic worldview. I drew inspiration from the story of how my parents met and the amount of discrimination and confusion both experienced when they decided to marry," Masri says. "I remembered my first day at grade school, feeling alienated and different from the rest of my classmates. I found that through telling my own stories, I could motivate others to do the same and allow them to come to their own realizations about others in the process."

As part of the project, Masri read his books to about two hundred children in seven very different elementary school classes in the Kansas City area, including rich upper class, Catholic, Islamic, inner city, and suburban schools. The purpose of the program was not only to quell discrimination of Arabs, but to

DESIGN CHALLENGE

Help prevent children from forming discriminatory stereotypes.

ENGAGEMENT STRATEGY

Building trust among young students and teachers by showing up at schools regularly and by keeping open channels of communication with the school administration.

DESIGN STRATEGY

Simplifying messages to concise, poetic metaphors so that young children learn how stereotypes can hurt people.

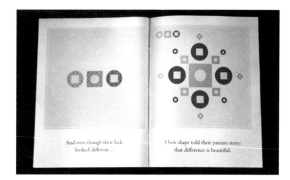

"I looked to El Lissitzky's *About 2 Squares* as a case study that illustrated how complicated problems could be articulated in simple and poetic ways. The universal implications of raw geometry had many interesting parallels to ideas of racial identity."

Ramzy Masri

OUTCOMES

About two hundred students participated in the reading program and exchanged correspondence with children from different schools, thereby increasing their exposure to new ideas and students of different backgrounds.

LESSONS LEARNED

Masri faced resistance from teachers and administrators early on and learned that it is important to clarify a project's intentions from the beginning.

Opposite
Masri's books are inspired by El Lissitzky, using geometric shapes to convey lessons about discriminatory stereotypes.

Above
Each student was paired and corresponded with another student in one of seven very different schools.

teach children the importance and beauty of difference. Discussing discrimination broadly allowed students to talk about being judged because of their weight, their size, how they talked, or the fact that they wore glasses. After reading his books to a class, Masri gave the students blank books to tell their own stories. Each child was then randomly paired with a "book pal" at a different school. The children swapped books, so that each student received a story from a child who came from a very different ethnic or social background. The final page in each book revealed the student's ethnic identity and where he or she went to school. The children then responded to their book pals and shared what they had learned during the project.

Although Masri considers A Book by Its Cover a success, it did not go exactly as he planned. "While my intent was for the children to author their own stories, many chose to tell these stories through metaphors. One example I recall," Masri says, "was by an eight-year-old boy who wrote a touching story about an apple not fitting in with a group of oranges. In some ways this was a breakthrough for me. While I was hoping that my assignment would be a kind of art therapy, I found that it was challenging the children to be communicators themselves: to take my call to action and author stories with the same sentiment I was advocating for: acceptance and curiosity towards people who are different from you." Another issue Masri faced was having to convince parents and teachers of the need to discuss these issues with children at such an early age. They were curious about why he wanted to talk about race and discrimination, but "Once I clarified my positive intentions, things went smoothly." Many schools Masri worked with had antibullying programs, so teachers saw his project as an extension of that curriculum.

A Book by Its Cover spawned many unlikely friendships. By the end of the project, students were exchanging phone numbers and Facebook information, teachers met each other, and volunteers worked with people from very different backgrounds. "I think this is the real outcome I hoped for in the beginning," Masri says. "Discrimination comes from a lack of real, physical connection with people who are different from you. For these children and adults to be making connections and friendships with people different from them—that's something that can make a difference." Masri succeeded not only in building trust with the students he was working with, but also in inspiring students to develop trusting relationships and build friendships with their peers beyond racial and social differences.

Promise Only What You Can Deliver

Avoid trying to solve all of the community's needs. While the community you work with may ask for a lot, you need to accurately estimate the time and resources that you can realistically contribute. Community development expert James Cavaye points to the "delineation of responsibility" as a key strategy to ensure that a project is efficiently carried out.[1] While he refers specifically to how government agencies engage communities, the same advice holds true for graphic designers who all too often try to create elaborate designs that deserve the attention of design armies.

The temptation to offer more may increase as you immerse yourself in a community and experience the needs up close. You may become as emotionally vulnerable as the people you want to help, and it might become difficult to say no to their requests, especially when your efforts have the potential to benefit individuals you have come to know personally. Social problems deserve realistic design solutions, however, and the community will not benefit from idealistic promises.

Understand the project's scope and be prepared to lower your expectations if an unforeseen development changes the parameters. As IDEO's Design for Social Impact: A How-To Guide advises, "Narrowing the scope of the project can often serve as an effective lever to increase efficiency."[2]

In other words, sometimes you need to avoid trying to invent grand solutions and be satisfied with what you can do in the time you have; it is up to you to figure out how much time and resources you can contribute. Make a list of the problems you see and identify what already exists in the community that you can build upon. Does the community have a service infrastructure, unique skills, or resources that you can utilize? Knowing your constraints and what you have to work with will help you determine what you can promise and how you can deliver.

The next two case studies feature projects by designers and students who worked effectively under constraints for two very different projects, a one-time event promoting local food and an ongoing podcast tour that explores the diversity of New York City's ecosystems.

Project Winterfood

Educating the public about the merits of buying and eating in-season, locally grown food

Despite our country's growing interest in local foods, many people still know little about its benefits and how they can make eating locally a practical part of an affordable lifestyle. A class of undergraduate students spent half a semester addressing this problem. According to Noah Scalin, their professor at Virginia Commonwealth University, "Corporate food producers dominate the messaging about healthy eating, and poorer communities are often stuck in food deserts where there is no access to healthy options."

Scalin's class, Design Rebels: Socially Conscious Graphic Design in Theory and Practice, challenges students to "create a project that reaches beyond the school walls and has a positive effect on their community." During the first half of the semester, Scalin's Design Rebels learn about the ethical issues that designers regularly face in their professional lives and have to consider how they would respond to each—such as whether or not they would take on an assignment that promotes an idea that they might not agree with, that marginalizes a group of people, or that causes unnecessary waste. Midway through the semester, each student proposes a socially conscious design project that incorporates

project WINTERFOOD

PROJECT WINTERFOOD IS A LOCAL FOOD EVENT AND ART EXHIBITION ORGANIZED BY A GROUP OF VCU GRAPHIC DESIGN STUDENTS. THE THEME OF THE EVENT IS SPINACH, APPLES, AND SWEET POTATOES— **ALL SEASONAL FOODS AVAILABLE IN VIRGINIA DURING THE WINTER.**

DEC 2ND
1509 W MAIN
7-10 PM

PROJECT DETAILS

DESIGNS Identity, booklets, exhibition, and related collateral

DATE August to December 2009

LOCATION Richmond, Virginia

LEADERS Noah Scalin (Virginia Commonwealth University)

DESIGNERS Fifteen students from Scalin's Design Rebels class, Virginia Commonwealth University

PARTNERS Central Virginia Food Bank, Gallery Five, Farm to Family Veggie Bus, Dominion Harvest, Savor Cafe, Ipanema Cafe, Rostov's Coffee & Tea, Ukrop's, the Byrd House Market

WEBSITE http://blog.alrdesign.com/2009/11/project-winterfood-december-2-richmond.html

specific community partners and is large enough for the entire class to complete in seven weeks with a starting budget of only one hundred dollars. One of these is then chosen for the class to work on through the end of the semester. Past projects promoted alternative transportation, raised money for a homeless shelter, and created an awareness campaign about resources available to abuse survivors in Richmond, among others.

"Projects often change or have to be reconfigured when the students realize how little time is truly going to be available," says Scalin, who considers teaching his students about realistic scheduling an important part of his class. His Design Rebels have only seven weeks to complete their project, although much community-based design work requires more time. Scalin shows his students how to establish a schedule and set appropriate

Previous page
Students designed the Winterfood promotional poster (detail seen here) as a call to action.

Below
The students highlighted grocery stores and restaurants that provide food from regional farms on a map.

Opposite
Promotional graphics for the Project Winterfood exhibition

Scalin shows his students how to establish a schedule and set appropriate parameters to complete their designs on time by working backward from a fixed deadline.

parameters to complete their designs on time by working backward from a fixed deadline. "Students are used to deadlines in school, but they really have no idea of what's involved in getting a large-scale, multicomponent project done," Scalin adds. "Everyone is used to waiting until the last minute to do assignments and then crams all night. Good scheduling skills are essential for getting client work done in the real world, especially if you work on multiple projects at the same time."

Scalin's fall 2009 class chose Project Winterfood, a proposal by student Christina Gleixner that focused on educating the local community about the merits of buying and eating in-season, locally grown food through an art and food exhibition and event. Once the topic was established, the class started to refine it and set about finding appropriate community partners—farmers, markets, and restaurants—who could contribute to the project. They worked in small groups, focusing on specific tasks, such as creating flyers, brochures, and posters to promote their event. Scalin explains that making mistakes is part of the learning process, and he steps in when the students head off course. "I required the smaller groups to give update reports each class period to the whole group and compare their status with their master calendar. That way they can quickly spot when things are heading off track, and I can help them with suggestions for how to reorganize themselves or rejigger their plans to keep things rolling."

In order to increase their initial budget of one hundred dollars, the students sold baked goods and handmade items at a local outdoor arts fair. A group of students created a hand-drawn logo as the centerpiece of their marketing campaign, while another group published a promotional blog for the exhibition and to raise awareness about local food. The class also solicited artwork to be sold at the event based on three locally available seasonal foods—apple, sweet potato, and spinach—and made a large map

DESIGN CHALLENGE
Creating an exhibition that communicates the benefits of local food in a compelling and empowering way.

ENGAGEMENT STRATEGY
Finding local community partners, such as farmers and food vendors, who agree to participate in and support the event.

DESIGN STRATEGY
Creating a variety of materials, such as flyers, brochures, and posters, whose design centers around a handmade logo.

"The students saw that they could create something real that could affect people in their community, and it gave them the confidence to do similar projects after they graduate."

Noah Scalin

OUTCOMES

The month-long exhibition about local food, farmers, and vendors attracted numerous visitors.

LESSONS LEARNED

A designer's expectations of a complex project should be scaled to fit a particular time frame by working backwards from the project's deadline and keeping the budget in mind.

of local resources that was put on display as well as booklets with information and recipes that were given to event visitors.

At the heart of the project was the collaboration with community partners: During the event, restaurants and a grocery store offered food samples featuring the winter foods apples, sweet potatoes, and spinach; the Farm to Family Veggie Bus, a mobile farmers' market bus, sold produce outside the event venue; and farm groups and CSAs set up tables to promote themselves. In addition, local bookstores donated cookbooks that were raffled away, and a local group of musicians performed at the event. The exhibit was very well attended, and a large number of artworks were sold. The profits were later donated to Central Virginia Food Bank, a local food bank, and Gallery 5, a community art gallery that hosted the art for a month.

While Scalin admits that "it is impossible to measure the actions that individuals took after attending the event (even a boost in CSA memberships and sales at the farmers' market could only speculatively be pinned on Project Winterfood and the efforts of these students)," he points out that the project was not only about changing the way people eat. "Just as important was that the students saw that they could create something real that could affect people in their community, and it gave them the confidence to do similar projects after they graduate." Working on a complex project that involved numerous community partners also taught them to be mindful of their time and resources when offering their help.

Opposite, top
Visitors were welcomed with this project overview, which highlights the students' mission, the benefits of local food, and their partners.

Opposite, bottom
Students organizing the exhibition

Above
Two students serve food made from locally sourced ingredients.

Right
Apples were among other fresh fruits and vegetables that doubled as decorations at the exhibition.

Safari 7

Exploring the complexity, biodiversity, conflicts, and potentials of New York City's ecosystems

Many New Yorkers use the subway to travel underground for miles at a time, remaining completely disconnected from the landscape they pass through. While city dwellers know the facts surrounding ecological issues of sustainability, recycling, and environmental awareness, they may not think of the city as part of an ecosystem in the same way as they would consider a natural landscape. The creators of Safari 7 started their project with the goal of educating city dwellers about the environment they pass through every day, pointing out to them how the city is intimately entwined with nature and encouraging them to fully embrace and participate in these important ecological issues. "The challenge is to help city dwellers see their immediate environment as urban nature, so they start to see the animals that co-inhabit our cities not as intruders but part of a larger ecosystem," says Glen Cummings of MTWTF.

A collaboration among architects, educators, and students at the Urban Landscape Lab at Columbia University, and graphic design studio MTWTF, Safari 7 is a self-guided tour of urban wildlife along the 7 subway line, a physical transect through New York City's most diverse range of ecosystems. Affectionately called the

Habitat

CORMORANT NESTING SITES

33 St – Queens Blvd

Vacant and Full

Vacant lots are left behind as neighborhoods change, old buildings are demolished, or new projects are put on hold. But vacant lots are anything but empty. With their protected edges, typical vacant lots in Queens host higher-than-average urban temperatures, creating subtle microclimates of sun and shade that attract migrating butterflies and small mammals. Lots are converted to local dumps or appropriated by neighbors to plant sunflowers and tomatoes (pollinated by butterflies) for the evening's salad course.

LISTEN IN: Steven Handel podcast series

PROJECT DETAILS

DESIGNS Podcasts, maps, subway tickets, website, stickers, exhibitions and supporting material; typeface: Neuzeit Grotesk

DATE Spring 2008–ongoing

LOCATION New York, New York

LEADERS Glen Cummings (partner, MTWTF, and lecturer, Yale University School of Art), Janette Kim, Kate Orff (codirectors, Urban Landscape Lab, Columbia University)

DESIGNERS More than thirty students and researchers (Urban Landscape Lab, Columbia University)

PARTNERS Metropolitan Transit Authority Arts for Transit; Graduate School of Architecture, Planning and Preservation, Columbia University; Studio-X New York; Studio-X Beijing; Queens Council on the Arts

WEBSITE www.safari7.org

"International Express," the 7 line runs from Times Square in Manhattan, under the East River, through a dispersed mixture of residences and parklands, ending in downtown Flushing, Queens, the nation's most ethnically diverse county. Subway riders can explore the complexity, biodiversity, conflicts, and potentials of New York's ecosystems by listening to podcasts and looking at maps that meld the city's ecological and urban characteristics. "We hope to engage the broadest range of New Yorkers, from commuters and schoolchildren to urban explorers and designers, in active research and exploration of their own environment," says Kate Orff, founder and codirector (with Janette Kim) of Columbia University's Urban Landscape Lab, who often looks for ways to "repurpose the city's infrastructure in order to rediscover and rethink it."

Safari 7 lets travelers experience train cars as eco-urban mobile classrooms and act as park rangers in their city. Many

Previous page
The team designed graphics that describe the landscape and history along the 7 train route.

Below
Students assemble a map for the exhibition, which shows the path along which the 7 train travels.

Opposite, top
Graphic describing the environment in Flushing, Queens

Opposite, bottom
Part of the finished exhibition map, which allows people to plug in to sections along the train route and learn about them

subway riders are already listening to their iPods while staring out the window. Now they can download podcasts with engaging content about the environment they pass through and reenvision their commute as a wildlife tour. The content, which ranges from information about local animals and plants to brief histories of specific sites, is generated by students in research seminars, by Urban Landscape Lab volunteers, and through interviews with experts, such as plant biologists, wild mushroom foragers, and local historians and foodies.

Cummings, Kim, and Orff brainstormed the idea for Safari 7 in 2008 with the concept of doing a guerrilla-type, low-budget project that would reach a broad audience and celebrate the complexities and potentials of nature in the city. With a great idea but no grant money in hand, they had to be efficient and flexible. As Cummings put it, "The euphemism 'doing more with less' implies that regardless of the parameters, a certain amount of design is required. My opinion is the exact opposite. Having less time and a lower budget means doing less design, and being comfortable with it. The challenge is to understand your resources and plan accordingly."

Partnerships, including collaborations with Metropolitan Transit Authority Arts for Transit, Studio-X New York, and the Queens Council on the Arts, who supported events and exhibitions,

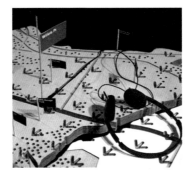

DESIGN CHALLENGE

Educating city dwellers about their immediate environment, so they start to see it as part of a larger ecosystem they need to protect.

ENGAGEMENT STRATEGY

Partnering with civic and municipal organizations to promote Safari 7.

DESIGN STRATEGY

Staying within a given budget by designing in a schematic way and scaling back expectations.

"Having less time and a lower budget means doing less design, and being comfortable with it. The challenge is to understand your resources and plan accordingly."

Glen Cummings

OUTCOMES

The team organized numerous guided tours on the 7 train and held an exhibition. Commuters can download the podcasts for self-guided tours from the Safari 7 website.

LESSONS LEARNED

The challenge of complex projects is to understand resources and plan accordingly.

helped the group create the many manifestations of Safari 7, from ad campaigns on the subway and Safari 7 MetroCard tickets, to a reading room exhibition and tours organized as part of the Queens Arts Express festival. "We design in a schematic way, then move right into production without dedicating a lot of time to visual refinement. As soon as something works, it's done. The Safari 7 exhibitions have a particularly diverse set of parts, and some are a bit rough," Cummings says. "This directness and diversity is one of the project's inherent visual qualities. It is born from necessity but it's also something we like a lot." The ecosystem growing out of the logo's Neuzeit Grotesk letterforms shows the directness of the group's approach and served as a style guide for other designs, from the podcast graphics to large exhibition maps.

The reaction has been very positive. A few thousand people have downloaded the podcasts, taken the self-guided tours, and attended exhibitions. The first Safari 7 tour included a small group of people who listened to the podcasts at various subway stops. Kim remembers a boy who was "a serious subway enthusiast. He had all the lines and stations memorized and paid close attention to each podcast throughout the trip. The next day we received an email from his mother with a photo of a homemade Safari 7 he had made. But when we looked closer, it wasn't for the 7 line, it was Safari 1 for the 1 line, the train he rides. We thought, 'Yes! That's it! Make your own Safari 7!' It's exciting for us that people use this project to start their own research and tell their own stories through Safari 7."

The team has begun to expand the vision of Safari 7 by collaborating with schools and transportation providers in Münster, Germany, and Beijing, China. Starting with a workshop in Beijing in June 2011, they have been working with local students and designers to explore transport lines, circulate pilot podcasts, and launch an exhibition. Using a method similar to Safari 7 in New York City, the team will partner with each city's transportation provider to present the podcasts on the train. "Our partners in these cities are revealing different cultural, environmental, and political attitudes toward nature in the city that are inspiring and eye-opening," says Kim.

Opposite, top
Safari 7 subway ads were displayed on number 7 trains.

Opposite, bottom left
A Safari 7 exhibition was held at Studio-X New York.

Opposite, bottom right
Safari 7 MetroCards advertised the project.

Below
Commuters on a guided tour

Prioritize Process

The sophistication of our world's visual culture continues to grow as immersive technology and interactive graphics become an increasingly large part of our lives. Creative tools have become intuitive enough for anyone with access to a computer to create a logo or a website, which may lead community members to form strong opinions about how graphics might help them solve their problems. Community leaders may show up to meetings with fixed ideas of what they want. These ideas, however, may be premature and lead designs in the wrong direction. To determine the best design solution, be prepared to address more fundamental questions about the community's needs before creating any graphics.

Following a standard design process that includes generating numerous ideas based on visual research, prototyping those ideas, and soliciting feedback from the target audience will give you an informed understanding of how design can play an important role in helping the community. As a designer you are equipped with a proven problem solving process and can tackle the issue with a fresh perspective.

The design teams working on the following two projects, Made in Midtown and projectOPEN, each followed a process that led to important realizations. Their design solutions are based on thorough research and provide novel approaches that address the fundamental needs of the communities with which they worked.

Made in Midtown

Exposing the stories that make the Garment District essential to Midtown Manhattan

More than a million New Yorkers pass through midtown Manhattan every day, but few realize that one of New York City's largest manufacturing clusters is located between thirty-fourth and fortieth streets. The midtown fashion industry contributes ten billion dollars to the city's economy every year,[1] and apparel manufacturing provides roughly 28 percent of New York City's manufacturing jobs.[2] The industry's presence also exerts a powerful influence on tourism, print and web media, education, film, and television.

However, in 2007 the Bloomberg administration announced that it was considering a proposal to lift the zoning restrictions that protect the Garment District's manufacturing spaces. Two years of negotiations between property owners, city officials, and fashion industry representatives had reached a stalemate, so in 2009 the Council of Fashion Designers of America (CFDA), a nonprofit trade association that leads industry-wide initiatives, asked the Design Trust for Public Space to develop a vision for the Garment District that allows manufacturing to coexist with residential and office space.

FASHION

IS BIG BUSINESS IN NEW YORK.
OF THE 70 FORTUNE 1000 COMPANIES HEADQUARTERED IN NEW YORK CITY, 9 ARE FASHION COMPANIES WITH A COMBINED YEARLY REVENUE OF

$31 BILLION

Source: Forbes, 2009

PROJECT DETAILS

DESIGNS Identity, website, pop-up exhibit, newspaper, tote bag; typefaces: Tungsten, Georgia
DATE September 2009 to May 2010
LOCATION New York, New York
LEADERS Megan Canning, Jerome Chou, and Deborah Marton (Design Trust for Public Space)
TEAM MEMBERS Glen Cummings (MTWTF); Daniel D'Oca, Georgeen Theodore, and Tobias Armborst (Interboro Partners); Sarah Williams (Columbia University's Spatial Information Design Lab); Jordan Alport; Tom Vanderbilt
PARTNERS Design Trust for Public Space, Council of Fashion Designers of America (CFDA)
WEBSITE www.madeinmidtown.org

The Design Trust for Public Space is an independent nonprofit organization dedicated to improving public space in New York City, soliciting projects that are timely, replicable, and relevant to the entire city, and that might create a ripple effect of influence on long-term design practice or public policy. In doing so the organization looks at problems in a holistic way, addressing the complete system instead of just one sector or part of the problem. As Design Trust's Deborah Marton puts it, "This story is not really about fashion. Made in Midtown is about what kind of city we want New York to be. It's about jobs and immigrant workers. It's about the decisions we make as a city to support one of the last neighborhoods in Manhattan that has not been remade by recent waves of new development."

For Made in Manhattan the organization defined the scope, budget, and timeline for the project. Design Trust staff does not produce actual design work. Instead, they partner with and build consensus between multiple stakeholders, conduct research, and manage a creative team that executes the deliverables. In this case they had to move fast. "We were under immense pressure to release our findings before the city made a decision about the zoning," says Megan Canning of Design Trust. "Our team began their research in January 2010, but needed to complete it by May 2010. If we didn't produce our study in time, the work would be useless."

Due to the time constraint the Design Trust decided to publish its findings as a website, since the web design and development could take place at the same time that the graphics were being produced. MTWTF partner Glen Cummings created a graphic identity based on Tungsten, a compact sans-serif typeface by Hoefler & Frere-Jones that he chose to fit a variety of formats, and collaborated with the interactive design firm Adapted Studio to build an information architecture that encouraged users to explore the site's content by thematic questions. Interboro Partners and Sarah Williams of Columbia University's Spatial Information Design Lab produced seventy-five quantitative and qualitative diagrams, maps, and infographics for the site, illustrating issues such as employment and land use. For this, Williams analyzed decades of industry data about zoning and real estate in the Garment District and the fashion industry's role in New York City's economy.

The Design Trust also recruited filmmaker Jordan Alport and journalist Tom Vanderbilt, who together spoke with more than seventy people at every level of the industry. Twelve video

A project of the Design Trust for Public Space
in partnership with the Council of Fashion Designers of America

Previous page
The design team created many graphics that illustrate the fashion industry's role in New York City's economy, including this one by Sarah Williams.

Above
The project identity, designed by Glen Cummings of MTWTF

Opposite
The modular project identity took on many forms, including large, vinyl lettering that promoted the initiative and advertised events.

interviews of designers, pattern makers, and retailers can be watched on the website and demonstrate how the fashion industry and the neighborhood matter to the city. As Marton explains, "These interviews showed us that the stakeholders had failed to connect industry data and trends to physical place; the value and success of this project was absolutely dependent on gaining their insights." According to her these stories are an "overwhelming resource that can tell us about the multifaceted dimensions of the communities we work with. The fashion community is no different—they were ready to tell us what makes them special; more importantly, they showed us who matters, from the person who sews a dress to the person that designs it."

Made in Midtown reached out to the general public with a two-day pop-up exhibit in a vacant storefront in the Garment District, a newspaper that was distributed around the neighborhood to commuters and industry workers, a limited-edition tote bag sold in designer boutiques across the city, and a short publication about this first phase of the project. In addition, the Design Trust organized lunchtime talks and public panel discussions that featured notable designers, planners, and city representatives.

Evaluating the project, Canning admits that the exhibit did not reach as many people as she had hoped, given the short time it was on view. She wishes the organization had enlisted more fashion students to distribute the newspapers throughout the neighborhood and arranged a public screening of Alport's videos. The first phase of Made in Midtown, however, has fulfilled its mission. Over ten thousand people from over eighty countries have spent an average of nearly eight minutes exploring the website since it launched. Made in Midtown convinced city officials and the public that the Garment District is a vibrant fashion research and development hub. As a result, the city withdrew its proposal to rezone the Garment District. *Crain's New York Business* credits Made in Midtown as the

DESIGN CHALLENGE
Telling the story of midtown Manhattan's fashion industry so that lawmakers, developers, and the public understand its importance to New York City and can have a productive conversation about how to develop the neighborhood.

ENGAGEMENT STRATEGY
Organizing a multidisciplinary team of creative individuals to research the fashion industry and tell its story in a compelling way.

DESIGN STRATEGY
Creating a website that is organized by thematic questions and provides a variety of information, including diagrams, maps, interviews, videos, and infographics.

"Stakeholders had failed to connect industry data and trends to physical place; the value and success of this project was absolutely dependent on gaining their insights."

Deborah Marton

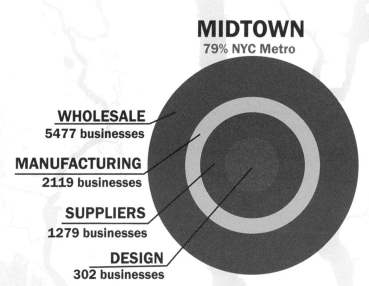

MIDTOWN
79% NYC Metro

WHOLESALE
5477 businesses

MANUFACTURING
2119 businesses

SUPPLIERS
1279 businesses

DESIGN
302 businesses

LONG ISLAND CITY
2% of midtown

LOWER MANHATTAN
7.6% of midtown

OUTCOMES

Over ten thousand people from over eighty countries spent an average of nearly eight minutes on the website, and the city put a hold on its plans to rezone midtown Manhattan.

LESSONS LEARNED

Made in Midtown was a success because the team's extensive research informed how they crafted and communicated the story of midtown Manhattan.

SUNSET PARK
2.5% of midtown

Opposite, top and middle
Forums helped educate the public about the
role midtown Manhattan plays in the fashion
industry. Events included screenings of videos
created by Jordan Alport. Visitors could also
buy Made In Midtown merchandise.

Opposite, bottom
This chart illustrates the different groups
that make up the fashion industry in midtown
Manhattan.

Above
The Made In Midtown website uses a modular
grid structure to organize the elements on
each page. The website includes interviews,
videos, and graphics to expose the real value
of midtown Manhattan's fashion industry.

tipping point in the city's decision to shelve its rezoning plans:
"Word of the city's move follows a study released this month by the
Design Trust for Public Space."[3]

As Steven Kolb of the CFDA puts it, "With this report,
for the first time all the different stakeholders in the Garment
District have nuanced and comprehensive information to
inform their opinions. We are all talking together as never
before to promote the concentration of creative industries that
is essential to the fashion ecosystem." According to Vanderbilt,
Made in Midtown's multidisciplinary approach played a big role
in its success. "I tried to tell the human stories and sketch a
portrait in words of who was in the district, how it works, and
how we should think about it, but I could never have expressed
the physical contours of the district, or the magnitude of its
physical change over the years, as effectively as Sarah Williams
did infographically; and I couldn't have captured the rich
visual anthropology and the process dynamics of the district
the way Interboro did with such clarity in its work; nor could I
have captured the kinetic energy or discrete personalities of its
participants the way Jordan did in his videography."

The many stakeholders who participated in the project have
asked the Design Trust to develop a convincing vision for future
planning in the Garment District. In Phase Two of the project the
organization will work with the CFDA and a team of private sector
Project Fellows to develop land use guidelines, programming, and
street-level interventions for the district's built environment that
position garment manufacturing as the core identity of a new
creative district.

projectOPEN

Designing a map that empowers Santa Monica's homeless population

HOMELESS SERVICES
RESOURCE GUIDE

Santa Monica

Homelessness affects nearly every city in the world, and the Los Angeles area is no exception. On any given night, fifty-one thousand people there are homeless.[1] In 2005 a group of design students at the University of California Los Angeles (UCLA) set out to address the problem in Santa Monica, a seaside city located along the western edge of Los Angeles that has long been known as the home of the homeless.

They started by researching the many causes of homelessness and meeting with members of forty-two organizations that assist the homeless population in Santa Monica. Their most important discovery was that most of the city's homeless organizations cater to a single issue, such as helping find a job or providing medical care. This confuses the homeless, many of whom do not know where to go for assistance. Many are also unsure or unaware of their basic human and civic rights. The students wanted to network with those organizations and help them communicate with one another, while reminding the homeless about their rights. Their solution was a homeless services resource guide called projectOPEN.

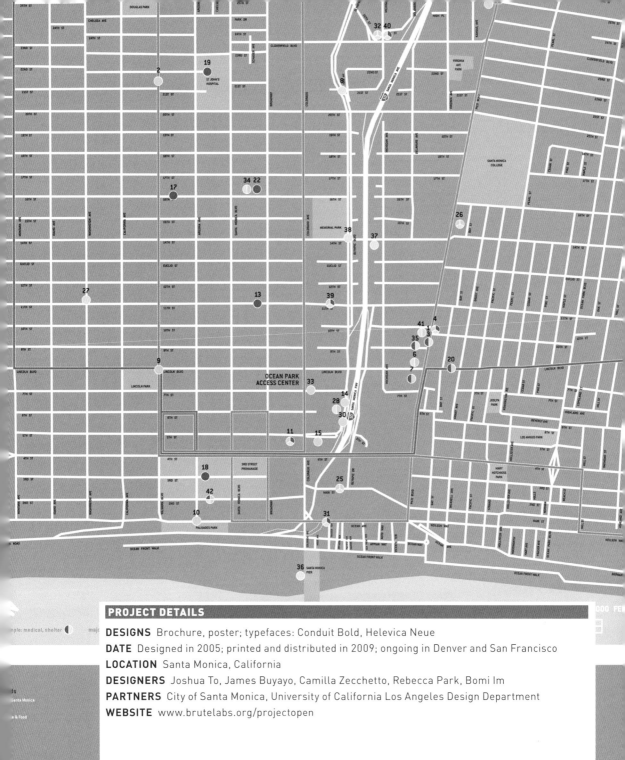

PROJECT DETAILS

DESIGNS Brochure, poster; typefaces: Conduit Bold, Helevica Neue
DATE Designed in 2005; printed and distributed in 2009; ongoing in Denver and San Francisco
LOCATION Santa Monica, California
DESIGNERS Joshua To, James Buyayo, Camilla Zecchetto, Rebecca Park, Bomi Im
PARTNERS City of Santa Monica, University of California Los Angeles Design Department
WEBSITE www.brutelabs.org/projectopen

16 Venice Family Clinic
Burke Health Center
2509 Pico Blvd, Santa Monica
(310) 392-8636

23 VA Homeless Access Center
West LA Veterans Admin Bldg #206
11301 Wilshire Blvd, West Los Angeles
(310) 268-4600

30 OPCC Youth Outreach Services *Night Light*
503 Olympic Blvd, Santa Monica
(310) 450-4050
Mon-Fri 9am-5pm, Sat 8am-12pm

37 Sunlight Mission
1754 14th St, Santa Monica
(310) 450-8802
Mon-Fri 9am-7pm, Sat-Sun 9am-4pm

The guide unfolds from a brochure into a large map that identifies valuable services, such as doctor's offices, shelters, social services, and food banks. Comprehensive information about each organization is printed below the map and includes the opening hours, contact information, and distinguishing facts, such as whether the organizations have a shower or if appointments are required. The back of the poster explains a homeless person's legal rights in Santa Monica, including issues such as solicitation, public behavior, camping in public parks, identification checks, and police searches. The students also listed safety tips and general advice that they distilled from their research, such as not wearing earplugs while sleeping in public and carrying a cheap watch to keep up to date about bus schedules or appointments. The map's design was inspired by the experiences of Santa Monica's homeless people: the colors

Previous page
The front side of the brochure serves as a map that highlights important services for the homeless population.

Below
The design unfolds to a poster.

mimic the light brown of dirt and sand, and the blue of the ocean and sky. The projectOPEN logotype sits within a curved rectangle reminiscent of an open park. Color-coded bus routes wind through the map, and the location of each organization follows a simple icon system that specifies what service it provides.

Santa Monica's city government initially agreed to pay for and distribute the map but reneged their offer when they saw the information about legal rights on the back of the poster. City officials have been trying to reduce the homeless population and were afraid that the map would go beyond helping Santa Monica's homeless population and attract even more homeless people to the city. The designers, however, believed that this information was essential for the homeless community and refused to remove it. The map went unprinted.

After graduating from UCLA, two students from the original group, Joshua To and James Buyayo, moved to San Francisco, where they helped start BRUTE LABS, a small studio that uses graphic design to address global challenges, such as poverty and health care. They worked on new initiatives but never forgot about projectOPEN. Four years after the map was first designed, they managed to convince the UCLA Art|Sci Center to finance the printing of both sides of the poster, and one thousand maps were subsequently distributed to homeless organizations throughout Santa Monica. To date there has been no rise in the homeless population.

BRUTE LABS has since been working on similar projectOPEN maps for San Francisco, where homelessness is especially prevalent. The San Francisco map will be trilingual in order to reach English-, Spanish-, and Chinese-speaking populations. The designers also want to coordinate a wayfinding system with the organizations featured on the map. Color-coded decals on front doors could help the homeless figure out which

The guide unfolds from a brochure into a large map that identifies valuable services, such as doctor's offices, shelters, social services, and food banks.

DESIGN CHALLENGE

Empowering Santa Monica's homeless population with information that can help improve their lives.

ENGAGEMENT STRATEGY

Interviewing Santa Monica's homeless population and the different organizations that support the homeless to understand their needs.

DESIGN STRATEGY

Allowing information gained during the research phase to guide the design. Being inspired by the prevailing colors of the places homeless people live in.

The designers could have buckled under the pressure of Santa Monica's city government and produced the map without including information on the homeless' legal rights, but they had learned during the research process how important it was for Santa Monica's homeless population to know their rights.

OUTCOMES

One thousand copies of the map were distributed among Santa Monica's homeless population. The project's success led BRUTE LABS to expand the project to new cities, including San Francisco and Denver.

LESSONS LEARNED

The students learned that it is important to keep funders and clients informed throughout the design process.

organizations offer shelter, food, medical, or social services. In addition, BRUTE LABS has plans for a web application that would allow anyone who has a smart phone help homeless people with directions and information.

With projectOPEN these designers took on an enormous challenge and made many good decisions during the course of the project. They consulted with organizations that were important to their research and made an effort to understand the breadth of homelessness. They let the voice of the homeless dominate the styling of the map and included controversial content that would help the community they were serving, and not their design careers. They helped homeless organizations coordinate efforts and work more collaboratively.

The designers could have buckled under the pressure of Santa Monica's city government and produced the map without including information on the homeless' legal rights, but they had learned during the research process how important it was for Santa Monica's homeless population to know their rights. This points to the importance of keeping the design process transparent, meeting with the community, clients, and funders frequently to keep everyone on the same page. The four-year lull between designing and producing the map might have been avoided if the designers had informed city officials early on about what they intended to include in their design. City officials might have denied the project right away and prompted the designers to look for another funding source.

Opposite
The back side of the poster outlines tips, rights, and responsibilities for Santa Monica's homeless population.

Above
The brochure fits into a brochure display case, which made it easy to distribute.

Right
The poster folds up into a brochure or can be rolled up into a tube.

Confront Controversy

Some projects deal with controversial subject matter. It is your job to address these issues, even if the community may not want to talk about them. Community members may be overly protective of certain topics or ashamed by the nature of their problems. Many of them may be in denial. Assess the purpose of the project you are working on and ask yourself if your design approach can disrupt the norm and make people change their behavior toward solving the problem.

Cynthia Hardy and Nelson Phillips, who study how organizations work, write about the value of creating conflict in order to disrupt cultural norms: "While collaboration can be highly productive in solving inter-organizational problems, conflict also has a clear role in challenging existing frameworks and forcing...change in directions considered by at least some members to be positive. Both aspects deserve equal attention, since failure to recognize the importance of conflict leads to a preference for the status quo and an implicit adoption of the viewpoint of powerful stakeholders."[1] These kinds of disruptions and changes do not need to take place overnight. As the Designers Accord Education Summit Toolkit advises, "When a pre-existing, hierarchical culture does exist, consider taking small steps versus initiating a culture shock."[2] Keep the target audience in mind. Establishing a level of trust and maintaining a good rapport with community members can determine the success of a campaign that deals with controversial topics.

Effectively confronting controversy is a tall order for a poster or website design. Survey community members and conduct focus groups to gauge their reactions to the problem. Use their insights and words to guide the project but bring in another perspective if needed. Meet with community partners frequently to make sure that your designs emphasize the outcomes that are needed in the community with taste and playfulness.

The next two projects, the Importance of Dialogue and Stories for the City, deal with controversy in very different ways, and their designers learn a lot in the process.

The Importance of Dialogue

Finding a way to talk about the controversial issue of predatory lending

In the past decade the highly contentious practices referred to as *predatory lending* have attracted the attention of industry analysts, economists, journalists, and both national and state lawmakers. To date, fifteen states prohibit one such practice—payday loans—outright, while others have passed caps with varying degrees of restriction.[1] The FDIC defines predatory lending as "imposing unfair and abusive loan terms on borrowers" and states that "such activities are inconsistent with safe and sound lending and undermine individual, family and community economic well-being."[2] In the fall of 2009 Professor Laura Chessin at Virginia Commonwealth University (VCU) challenged her senior graphic design students to consider some of the complex issues surrounding this issue, such as banking deregulation and compounded interest rates, lobbying, and legislation.

      With government regulation of health care and economic uncertainty foremost in the press, Chessin decided to engage her students with the issue of spiraling poverty in the urban community surrounding the VCU campus in Richmond, Virginia. She met with Jay Speer and Dana Wiggins from the Virginia Poverty

AUTO-PAWN OF AMERICA, INC.

WHERE YOUR PAWNS ARE /// FAST CASH

804-233-PAWN (7296) CASH FOR GOLD

AUTOPAWNOFAMERICAINC.COM

6029

U-HAUL

STORAGE ROOMS

CUSTOM HITCHES

PROJECT DETAILS

DESIGNS Posters
DATE Fall 2009
LOCATION Richmond, Virginia
LEADERS Laura Chessin (Virginia Commonwealth University)
DESIGNERS Fourteen graphic design students (Virginia Commonwealth University)
PARTNER Virginia Poverty Law Center

Law Center (VPLC) to learn more about their work advocating for regulatory action with the upcoming Virginia General Assembly. Both were eager to bring in the creative energy of design students to help garner support for their campaign.

Early in the semester Speer and Wiggins, armed with fact sheets, statistics, and policy statements, held a presentation for the class, explaining the two types of predatory loans that were addressed in the proposed legislation: payday loans (short-term loans meant to cover a borrower's expenses until the next payday) and car title loans (a car's title and a copy of the car's keys are given to the lender in exchange for the loan). Speer presented interviews with desperate borrowers who had to decide between paying off a loan and having cash to cover living expenses. The stories included accounts of escalating intimidation and loss of property.

The students returned to class the next week with a range of responses. Some said that they distrusted Speer's passionate rhetoric, while others blamed borrowers for their ignorance, poor budgeting, and overconsumption. "At one point," Chessin noted, "it seemed that the project was in mutiny. I had to step in and ask students to carefully examine their preconceptions,

It took conflict in the classroom for Chessin to recognize the necessity for a broader contextual framework to address the cultural and political landscape of poverty.

Previous spread, opposite, and above
Students documented the many forms of
predatory lending as part of their research.

attitudes, and assumptions." In an effort to encourage them to think critically about topics of class and poverty, she introduced an exercise from her course in women's studies that addresses issues of race, class, and gender politics by examining assumptions. Defining assumptions as "what we hold to be true based on opinion, prejudice, personal experience and often learned from our environment (family, peer, community), yet lacking supporting quantitative or qualitative evidence," she asked students to identify what purpose particular assumptions serve. In the context of gender studies, students would most often explore how assumptions perpetuate an imbalance of power across race, class, and gender. When her students identified the assumptions they had brought to the predatory lending project, the list included such statements as, "The folks taking out loans are materialistic consumers buying expensive cars," and "They're lazy and don't want to work." Many of the students worked part-time to cover school expenses or had taken out loans themselves, and expressed little compassion for the stories of economic hardship, characterizing consumers facing mounting debt as "living irresponsibly."

The breakthrough came when one student pointed out that "we're either blaming the people who take out loans for being irresponsible or blaming the lenders for entrapment." Another student added, "There doesn't seem to be any middle ground or room for conversation." The ensuing discussion included topics such as problems faced by single-parent families, the lack of education for parts of the population, and concerns about home ownership (and foreclosure) and employment prospects. Through the course of this dialogue, the class as a group began to see the complexity of the issue. Given the task to define the goal of the project, they agreed that it needed to both educate the consumer and promote a discussion among lawmakers. Instead of backing down from the topic's controversy, the class learned how to talk

DESIGN CHALLENGE

Creating a productive dialogue around the contentious issue of predatory lending.

ENGAGEMENT STRATEGY

Partnering with a nonprofit organization that dedicates its resources to informing the population about high-risk loans. Addressing and overcoming personal prejudices through research.

DESIGN STRATEGY

Designing posters in a range of styles to educate the public and draw sympathy from lawmakers.

2/3

OF PAYDAY LOANS ARE MADE TO FAMILIES HEADED BY SINGLE MOTHERS

NATIONALLY 2/3 of payday loans are taken by households headed by single mothers. Often, these families are those moving from the welfare category to the working category and half of these families have multiple children under the age of 18. When taking a payday loan these families DOUBLE their chances of filing for bankruptcy. Even when compared to families in similar financial distress who might have been denied a loan.

Above
Poster by Steven Conaway

Left
Poster by Jacob Elliot

Opposite, top
Poster by Alec Catalano

Opposite
Poster by Eva Kamieniak

OUTCOMES

The posters were displayed in Virginia's General Assembly Building during the legislative session.

LESSONS LEARNED

The students learned to evaluate their prejudices when dealing with contentious issues.
Their instructor learned the importance of bringing other perspectives into the classroom.

Chessin challenged her students to design posters that demonstrated their take on the issue of predatory lending based on their research and dialogue.

about it and, as a result, created designs that cut through the rhetoric surrounding predatory lending and promoted dialogue.

Chessin challenged her students to design posters that demonstrated their take on the issue of predatory lending based on their research and dialogue. The students responded with two general approaches, either communicating what predatory lending is or depicting a scenario that attempted to draw sympathy (or empathy) from their audience. Their styles ranged from handwritten to the use of photographic material or digital illustrations.

When Speer and Wiggins returned for a final critique, they were excited by the students' work. Chessin, who had been concerned that they would be disappointed that the designs were not more aggressive and confrontational, was surprised at how supportive and receptive the clients were to rethinking their tone and message. The project thus informed not only the students and their audience, but the VPLC as well. The posters were displayed at a public reception and then employed to promote dialogue among lawmakers and lobbyists inside the General Assembly Building during the legislative session.

Looking back, Chessin admits that it took conflict in the classroom for her to recognize the necessity for a broader contextual framework to address the cultural and political landscape of poverty. In retrospect she wishes she had invited a sociologist to talk about policy debates and social welfare, as "Interdisciplinary approaches help students recognize that graphic design is not a delivery so much as it is an invitation to research and engage."

Stories of the City

Creating a sense of community through graphic interventions

In our age of social networks, many of us are in touch daily with people from around the world, but few of us actually know our next-door neighbors. "There is a clear lack of community, solidarity, and interpersonal interaction with people we regularly see," Tyler Galloway, assistant professor in graphic design at the Kansas City Art Institute (KCAI), claims. "Life would be richer and safer if we had deeper, ongoing relationships with those in close proximity to us." He attributes this lack of interaction to many complex sociological factors, such as the fact that the average American spends 8.5 hours in front of television and computer screens, and more time at work than citizens of most other developed countries.[1, 2] Transience, city planning, and patterns in commerce also play a role.

In the spring of 2008, Galloway decided to focus on the issue with his students in a class called "Stories of the City," aimed at exploring "how narrative design can create a sense of community, solidarity, and interpersonal interaction." This was done primarily through a series of designer-initiated, community-focused projects in which students engaged otherwise anonymous neighbors. Projects ranged from working with a knitting group and

GOOD
NEIGHBORS
MAKE GREAT
PEOPLE.

PROJECT DETAILS

DESIGNS Booklet, installation, slideshow; typeface: Cellini
DATE January to May 2008
LOCATION Kansas City, Missouri
LEADERS Tyler Galloway (Kansas City Art Institute)
DESIGNER Morgan Ashley Allen (Kansas City Art Institute)

local vegetarians, to getting together neighborhood residents. The first step was to choose a group or neighborhood to work with.

Sophomore Morgan Ashley Allen took the most direct approach to Galloway's challenge by trying to create community within Columbus Park, an old neighborhood in Kansas City, where she lives. Allen wanted to foster a dialogue between her neighbors, though she was initially at a loss for how to do this. "*Community* isn't something you can look at, and this makes it hard to talk about," Allen says. "It means different things to different people. The biggest breakthrough I had was realizing that this was holding me back."

The students spent several weeks trying to get to know their groups, making relationship charts to map their research and all of the people they met. They found it difficult to make the initial connection, though, as most people simply ignored any requests for interaction. Allen started her project by designing a questionnaire that portrayed her honest intent to befriend her neighbors, putting it through the mail slots in her building, so her neighbors would notice it as soon as they got home. "I asked casual questions. Things I would ask if passing in the hall: How long have you been in our building? What brought you here? How do you feel about the neighborhood and what would you like to improve?" About five of the forms were returned to her with semifriendly responses that did not have much information

"Community isn't something you can look at, and this makes it hard to talk about. It means different things to different people."

Morgan Ashley Allen

Previous spread
Allen gave this poster to her neighbors in an attempt to foster a sense of community.

Opposite
Allen projected images of neighborhood houses on a wall of an abandoned buidling to elicit responses from her neighbors.

Top
Allen's research distilled into an end-of-semester installation

Above
Galloway takes his classes on immersive trips into the community at the start of each semester.

on them. "No one really poured their heart out to me or seemed interested in continuing a conversation on a more intimate level," she says. "One guy was actually angry that I contacted him and took the time to fill out one of the questionnaires. He didn't answer any of my questions, but he gave me a very lengthy explanation as to why he didn't want me putting things in his mailbox."

Most students soon began to focus on creating connections between people with common interests rather than geographic proximity or to utilize known networks of people. Projects began to shift significantly, becoming more successful after that point. "This showed me that our society generally prioritizes relationships based on shared likes rather than geography," Galloway says. Despite Allen's disheartening first attempt to create community, she continued to use guerilla tactics to prod her neighbors. She carried the look and feel of the questionnaire, which was set in Cellini, a typeface designed by Albert Boton, into other parts of the project so it would be understood as a cohesive system. One part of this system was a set of forty small booklets that each unfolded into a poster to be hung in a window, a way for neighbors to signal that they had responded to Allen's project. The pages featured black-and-white images of neighborhood houses and simple, disarming phrases such as "Love your neighbor," "Let me know if you ever need any help," and "Your dog is really cute." The books, which the student hand-delivered to her neighbors, also included small messages that could be torn away and given to a neighbor, such as "Thanks for the cup of sugar." Allen subsequently saw three posters hung in the windows of her neighbors' apartments.

Allen used the same images of houses, combined with the message of "Love your neighbor," in a slideshow that she projected on the side of an abandoned building in her neighborhood. She wanted to draw people out of their apartments and give them a reason to interact. "My main hope was that the images would spark a response,

DESIGN CHALLENGE
Creating stronger communities with designs that incorporate narratives from members of those communities.

ENGAGEMENT STRATEGY
Using guerilla tactics to prod community members.

DESIGN STRATEGY
Creating a cohesive set of materials to encourage Columbus Park residents to interact with each other.

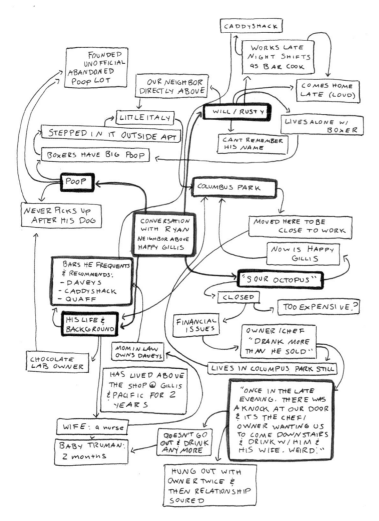

"A designer needs a solid point of entry into a community to have credibility and trust with them."

Tyler Galloway

OUTCOMES

No substantial connections were made, and Allen did not grow much closer to anyone in her community, though both she and Galloway discovered important aspects of working with communities.

LESSONS LEARNED

Allen learned that the collaboration of community members is extremely important. Without their support, a project can easily fail. Building trust can help encourage them to participate even in controversial projects.

Above and opposite, right
Allen created and distributed a booklet with images, neighborly messages, and a tear-away poster.

Opposite, left
As part of their assignment, Galloway required his students to create a relationship map that charted their immersive experiences.

such as "Oh, that's my house! I wonder what this is all about," she says. "If they didn't stop to chat, I hoped they would at least see the main message and think about it." Allen kept the images black and white to create enough contrast for the projection and to maintain a visual consistency. "It was an empty lot, and the show only lasted one night. There was some animosity about having the right to inhabit the space, so I didn't feel comfortable doing it longer."

Allen admits that the directness of her approach did not yield any significant results. "My immediate next-door neighbors talked to me a little about my project, but most of them were unsure of the project or how they could contribute. As far as they were concerned, they were happy with the condition of their community and didn't share my concerns or advocacy." While neighborhood cohesion might not seem like a controversial issue, Allen learned that asking strangers to become involved in her project did not lead to the outcome she had hoped for. Establishing a level of trust and maintaining a good rapport with her neighbors before asking for their participation might have yielded better results.

Galloway learned a similar lesson. "The major problem of the class was the way I framed the project," he admits. "I assumed that people would be open to meeting their physical neighbors and to create community with them. I also assumed a certain boldness or activist-type attitude from the students, which wasn't necessarily there, or had to be developed. If I ran the class in the future, I would encourage students to cast a wider net and to talk to multiple communities. I would also encourage them to work with a familiar community or person as an entry point to their project. I would assign communities to groups of students, rather than expecting everyone to work alone; a designer needs a solid point of entry into a community to have credibility and trust with them." For Galloway's visual advocacy class, which all KCAI graphic design majors take, he has "begun to work with specific community partners, which my colleague and I contact before the class starts," as he explains. "This gives students some focus, rather than allowing them to start off in any random direction for their work."

STRENGTH

Identify the Community's Strengths

Consider the community's unique challenges with sensitivity. It is easy to draw attention to a problem by highlighting its shocking details, but this often involves using compromising imagery that treats people as objects of pity, doing little to improve their self-esteem. "There is a tendency to emerge from a community process with a heavy emphasis on problems," states Prevention By Design.[1]

Instead of focusing only on a community's shortcomings, chart both its strengths (local language, style, skills) and challenges (literacy levels, drug and crime problems) and use that list as a guide throughout the project. Take inspiration from your interactions with community members and find ways to create an emotional tie with the general public by representing them with dignity.

Work with community leaders to identify the resources and assets that you can mobilize to solve the community's problems. Show community members why they are unique and valuable, in order to help them develop social capital that can help them productively engage with the world around them.[2]

The following two projects, Reason to Give and Es Tiempo, show how design teams can take an active role in identifying and highlighting a community's strengths and make use of them in their design solutions.

POVERTY

Reason to Give

Encouraging locals to help their neighbors in need

The Chicago neighborhood of Humboldt Park is becoming increasingly diverse, but the gentrification of the largely Hispanic community comes at a price. Civic organizations, such as the Puerto Rican Cultural Center and the Humboldt Park Empowerment Partnership's Housing Action Team, point to the influx of developers buying blighted real estate and the construction of luxury condominiums as the main reasons why low-income families can no longer afford the neighborhood's increasing rents and property taxes. Longtime residents are forced to move to different communities, and the Anti-Hunger Federation has noticed that donor organizations have provided fewer resources that meet the basic needs of Humboldt Park residents.

Firebelly Design, a graphic design studio that sits in the heart of Humboldt Park, recognized this growing problem in 2007. As Firebelly Design founder Dawn Hancock explains, her team has created "Good Design for Good Reason"—the studio's tag line—since 1999, but "While good design can change hearts and minds, we know profound world change requires getting out and getting involved." To this end, she started the initiative Reason to Give, the

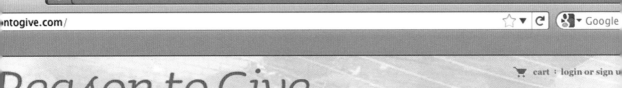

of... +

ntogive.com/ ☆ ▼ C 🔧 ▼ Google

Reason to Give

🛒 cart : login or sign u

bout : Give : Humboldt Park : Success Stories : For Sponsors : Apply

Reason To Give is
a storefront of Humboldt Park's
basic needs.

Hear their stories, donate directly
and change someone's life.

Certificate
Any amount donated

Certificate + T-shirt
$20 or more donation

Certificate + T + To
$100 or more donatio

ind a Reason to Give!

Donate Any Amount!
$ [   ] **Give ▶**

Holiday Gift Cards
a great way to give

Happening Now!

Reason to Give and
Feltpad Host
Chicago Code

s that time again: Back to School!
his year we are offering a two-day
omputer programming workshop at
...stars for teens. The workshop will
e beneficial... +more

Reason to Give
adopts our next
on-profit: Ru
rts Center!

umble Arts came to Reas
ve because they need he
ering scholarships to you
ant to participate in their S
ts Camp but cannot... +m

Previous news & even

Reasons To Give... *Those Who Need*

Mother needs help providing for her youngest daughter

- -

88% given ▬▬▬▬▬▬▬▬▬▬▬ ▶ Give Now

PROJECT DETAILS

DESIGNS Website, promotional collateral; typeface: Sauna
DATE 2007–ongoing
LOCATION Chicago, Illinois
LEADER Dawn Hancock (Firebelly Foundation)
DESIGNERS Dawn Hancock and Will Miller (Firebelly Design)
PARTNER Firebelly Foundation
WEBSITE www.reasontogive.com

ults,

ewsletter

Boots for kids

ail [   ]

premier project of Firebelly Foundation, a nonprofit offshoot of the studio, with the goal of meeting the immediate needs of Humboldt Park residents. Reason to Give started as an open-ended concept—finding out how to help. Hancock and her coworkers realized that it would be difficult to carve out their niche in the community. "Humboldt Park is full of well-established organizations," Hancock says. "It's hard to start a new initiative and gain the trust of both those you are trying to serve and those you are hoping will donate. We're a group of young Caucasians asking families in a predominately Latino and African-American community to let us into their homes and to some extent their lives. This takes a great amount of cultural sensitivity." In order to make sure that their solutions became sustainable, the Firebelly team worked closely together with the Puerto Rican Cultural Center and numerous churches and community organizations.

The designers hit the streets to document the neighborhood with illustrations, photography, and video. They wanted to avoid giving the impression that they had all the answers. Instead, they proceeded to ask a lot of questions and

Previous spread
The Reason to Give homepage allows donors to seach by type of need, its cost, or a specific recipient.

Above and below
Every family that requests assistance from Reason to Give is given an online profile that includes professional photographs.

"It's hard to start a new initiative and gain the trust of both those you are trying to serve and those you are hoping will donate. We're a group of young Caucasians asking families in a predominately Latino and African-American community to let us into their homes and to some extent their lives. This takes a great amount of cultural sensitivity."

Dawn Hancock

created a dialogue that showed that they were serious, dedicated, and willing to do whatever it took, "even if it meant scrapping our entire idea for something completely new." Their research helped the team understand the lives, situations, and needs of residents, schools, and local organizations. "You gain a new kind of respect for people who are willing to share with you, and you begin to really see the strength of the community," states Hancock.

While many people consider only food and water to be basic needs, their research led the Firebelly designers to believe that winter gear, shoes, school supplies, bedding, kitchen appliances, and computers are equally important. According to Chicago's former mayor Richard Daley, "In the twenty-first-century economy, everyone needs to have access to computer technology to succeed in life. Computer literacy is a fundamental skill in the modern world."[1] In order to meet some of these basic needs, Hancock decided to create a web store where donors can purchase items for the Humboldt Park community.

The designers sampled colors that captured the look and feel of the neighborhood and developed ideas for the homepage. After settling on a wireframe structure, they built subpages using Underware's Sauna typeface as the header, and loaded them with information, soliciting feedback throughout the process. "After the site was live for six months, we realized we needed to change the focus of the homepage to showcase not only the needs of the community, but also the successes made possible through the donations, and to give people more options to donate—some people wanted the family to decide what they needed most," Hancock explains. The website had gone live so quickly that it had outgrown itself after only a short time, and additional web tools also became necessary. "In hindsight, a more robust content management system would have been useful to implement along with the first launch of the site," Hancock admits.

DESIGN CHALLENGE

Helping families in need by connecting them with people who want to give but do not know how.

ENGAGEMENT STRATEGY

Immersing themselves into the Humboldt Park community by documenting the neighborhood and asking a lot of questions to find out how best to help.

DESIGN STRATEGY

Sampling the community's style as inspiration for the website. Framing the needs of people with dignity by featuring them in videos and photographs, and giving them an opportunity to talk openly about their needs.

Left
Each family has a profile page that lists the items it needs, how much they cost, and how much has been donated so far.

Opposite, top and middle
In addition to creating the website, Firebelly Foundation also brought together donations for a holiday party.

Opposite, bottom
Donors receive a certificate of thanks that lists what they gave and how it contributed to helping a particular family in need.

OUTCOMES

The needs of many families have been met by Reason to Give since 2007. Donations doubled in 2009 and again in 2010. Over forty-five volunteers have contributed over three thousand hours and the website reaches about two thousand hits a month.

LESSONS LEARNED

The designers learned that it makes sense to create a robust content management system for a website from the start of the project.

The Reason to Give online storefront makes donating simple and direct for the pool of donors who would like to help the community but do not know how to. The website features video interviews with community members explaining what they need most, and visitors can choose to donate toward those needs from a list of basic items purchased from responsible retailers and sustainable manufacturers. Donors can return at a later time to watch a follow-up video.

The site does not only encourage people to help but also gives members of the Humboldt Park community an outlet to tell their stories to the rest of the world. The neighborhood is too often in the news for its high rates of violence and crime, but it is also home to beautiful parks and wonderful people. The site's video interviews create a human connection between the donor and the recipient. Instead of showing community members in desperation, the videos portray them with dignity, giving them a place to express themselves. Hancock points to the initiative's first success as her most memorable: providing all new winter gear to a young girl in the neighborhood who wanted "a puffy, puffy coat, like Santa."

Reason to Give has been made possible by Firebelly Foundation's strong network of volunteers, corporate givers, and the members of the new middle class who are moving into the community. The program also has a loyal base of individual donors that expands beyond the neighborhood's borders. The initiative has made a huge impact in the Humboldt Park community. Individual donations doubled in 2009 and then again in 2010. To date, Reason to Give has helped fulfill the needs of over six hundred community members, one organization, and two local schools. The program has attracted over forty-five committed volunteers, who have dedicated over three thousand hours. Traffic to the website has reached over two thousand hits per month in just two years due to social media, networking, and media coverage.

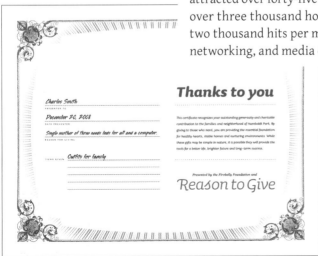

Es Tiempo

Encourage Los Angeles's Latina
population to attend annual Pap tests in
an effort to prevent cervical cancer

Hispanic women have the highest incidence and mortality rates for
cervical cancer of any major racial or ethnic group in the United
States.[1] While case studies show that the best way to prevent and
detect cervical cancer is with annual Pap tests, many Hispanic
women do not go to the gynecologist regularly. A group of students
at Art Center College of Design's Designmatters department saw this
as an opportunity for a design campaign dedicated to convincing
the Latina community of the importance of annual Pap tests.

   Mariana Amatullo, vicepresident and cofounder of
Designmatters, helped shape the project in keeping with the
school's mission to engage, empower, and lead an ongoing
exploration of art and design as a positive force in society.[2]
The group of seven students, led by professors Elena Salij and
Maria Moon, included graphic designers, photographers, fine
artists, and illustrators, who teamed up with Dr. Robert Haile at
the USC Norris Comprehensive Cancer Center as a partner. He
became the primary visionary leader for the project, assembling
a team of medical providers, clinicians, and educators who
served this particular population. Together, they acted as the

PROJECT DETAILS

DESIGNS Posters, credit card, stickers, labels, signage, website, video, murals; logotype: Gill Sans
DATE June to August 2009
LOCATION Los Angeles, California
LEADERS Elena Salij and Maria Moon (Designmatters, Art Center College of Design)
DESIGNERS Seven students (Designmatters, Art Center College of Design)
PARTNER University of Southern California (USC) Norris Comprehensive Cancer Center, USC Keck School of Medicine, USC Annenberg School for Communication and Journalism
WEBSITE www.designmattersatartcenter.org/proj/es-tiempo

students' expert consultants throughout the project, starting with a lecture by Haile, who taught the group about the medical procedures that women go through.

Another important collaboration was with Dr. Sheila Murphy, professor at the USC Annenberg School for Communication and Journalism, who helped the students communicate effectively with their target audience and develop questions for focus groups, an essential step of their research process. These questions aimed at learning about the attitudes of community members and the barriers that prevent these women from going for a Pap test. "Their answers were contrary to our assumptions," Moon explains. "We initially thought that this particular group of women might not be aware that they needed to get a Pap smear regularly. Then the design problem would have been a matter of education. But what we found was that these women *knew* that they needed to get a Pap smear done but didn't realize the importance of having it done annually. Not only did the women need some sort of reminder, many could not afford to take the time off, a totally different design problem altogether." After evaluating the results of the focus groups, the students decided

"When we heard all of the barriers that prevented women from going to Pap tests, our inital ideas of how to solve the problem were blown right out the door."
Maria Moon

Previous spread
The Es Tiempo awareness campaign included
large wall graphics.

Above
The design team

Opposite and below
Results from focus group sessions in which
Latina women were asked for ideas that might
attract other women to get their Pap smears

to narrow their target audience to those women with the least
access to, knowledge of, or ability to navigate the health care
system. This, they believed, was where design had the potential to
make the broadest impact. "When we heard all of the barriers that
prevented women from going to Pap tests, our initial ideas of how
to solve the problem were blown right out the door," Moon admits.

One of the students' initial ideas was to create a campaign
that loudly proclaimed, "Get Your Pap Smear Today!," with colorful
posters, decorated bus stops, and a Pap-test-mobile. "We thought the
message needed to be loud and clear," Moon says. "What we found
was that discretion was more valued than proclamation." Another
campaign idea would have featured a Hispanic woman doctor, but
it turned out that many of the women did not trust doctors. It
became clear that the message, language, and all the visuals in the
campaign needed to work toward establishing this trust.

The students also realized that they would have to navigate
the prevailing cultural stigma about cervical cancer. "An elaborate
integrated communications campaign—knocking down as many
barriers as possible—was required," Moon explains. Repeated
brainstorming, ideation, rapid prototyping, and evaluation helped
the designers clarify their message, expose weaknesses in specific
ideas, and find possible solutions while maintaining consistency
and identifying opportunities to strengthen their campaign. The
final solution focused on the positive aspects of prevention rather
than the negative consequences of inattention.

The picture of a Jacaranda tree, whose large, purple flowers
are a prevalent and welcome sight in Southern California every
spring, became the project's visual identity. The students adapted
the visual styling of the tree for each of their designs, which
included maps and environmental graphics, such as posters,
billboards, and murals, that directed women to the nearest clinic
with an informal script typeface: "*Es importante. Es facil. Es tiempo.*

DESIGN CHALLENGE

Raising awareness among Latina
women about the importance of
getting an annual Pap smear to
prevent cervical cancer.

ENGAGEMENT STRATEGY

Partnering with local hospitals
and research groups to learn how
to craft the message in a way that
addresses the issues effectively
and with sensitivity. Conducting
focus groups to learn about the
concerns and strengths of the
community.

DESIGN STRATEGY

Building the campaign around
the picture of a Jacaranda tree
to inspire trust among the target
audience.

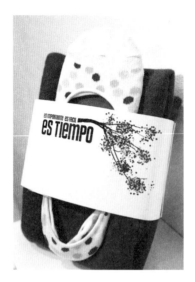

Top, left
The students designed slippers and a medical gown using the Jacaranda pattern.

Top, right
They teamed up with VISA to help Latina women pay for the time they would need to take off from work to get their Pap smears.

Left
Paper covering for the exam table

Opposite, top
Billboard featuring the project tagline, "Es importante, es facile, es tiempo"

Opposite, middle
The students also designed maps for bus shelters that list doctors in different neighborhoods.

Opposite, bottom
Bus ads promote the project.

OUTCOMES

Students produced a system of designs that encourage Hispanic women in Los Angeles to get their annual Pap tests.

LESSONS LEARNED

The results of focus groups indicated that the Latina community would not respond to messages that are too direct. Instead the team used more personal language and imagery that was familiar to the community.

It's important. It's easy. It's time." As Moon explains, "What these women needed was a sister, cousin, or friend reminding them that there was nothing to be afraid of and that they need to make an appointment." The students steered away from making their designs look overtly Hispanic. "We found that our audience is sensitive to brands and design, and they weren't necessarily interested in being singled out. If anything they wanted to be treated equally," Moon recalls.

As part of the project, the students devised an incentive to ease the financial burden of missing work in order to get tested: the Es Tiempo VISA gift card. These cards would be credited with cash that could be spent anywhere. An Es Tiempo line of products would help subsidize the program, with corporations committed to women's health, such as OPI and Avon, manufacturing and selling these products and sharing their profits.

As a final step, the students created a kit that helps women feel more comfortable at clinics that are part of the Es Tiempo campaign. "It became clear that our campaign could not just usher women into terrifying exam experiences," Moon says. The kit includes removable stickers to keep hospital gowns closed, a lap blanket to keep women's legs warm before and after the Pap test, and slippers.

Designmatters and its partners intend to launch an integrated media campaign of Es Tiempo in Los Angeles county that will build on the existing infrastructure and relationships of the USC Norris Comprehensive Cancer Center, including partnerships with twenty-five health clinics in Los Angeles county that provide Pap tests and the Cancer Detection Programs: Every Woman Counts's hotline.

Utilize
Local Resources

The connectedness of the community you work with will be its greatest resource. As Cavaye points out, helping a community address its needs should not "undervalue the existing often informal capacity of communities."[1]

Talk to community leaders and survey the community to determine what local material resources are plentiful and can be incorporated into the design. Learn what skills or talents community members might contribute during the research process and to the final design solution. Utilize these resources to create a design that more effectively integrates into their lives and that empowers them to deal with similar issues in the future.

Wet Work and Keys for the City are two projects that integrate local resources and show how such use can increase a design's connection to the community.

Wet Work

Using local resources to talk about Chicago's (mis)use of water

The flow of the Chicago River was reversed in 1900, when it was connected to the Mississippi River via the sanitary and ship canal. [1] Until then the water withdrawn from Lake Michigan for Chicago's water supply had been replenished by the river and returned to the Great Lakes. Now approximately 2.1 billion gallons of fresh water are diverted out of the Great Lakes Basin every day. Over one billion gallons of that water goes to Chicago residents, and, after being used and treated, ends up in the Mississippi River before draining into the Gulf of Mexico. [2] This profound loss of a cherished resource motivated Moving Design—a group of sixteen designers, architects, street artists, educators, and an engineer—to draw attention to the problem in the summer of 2010. They gathered for twelve evenings to develop ways to broadcast facts about Chicago's water usage that would penetrate neighborhoods and galvanize residents to act on the information.

Rick Valicenti and John Pobojewski founded Moving Design in 2009 to "inspire and elevate the culture of communication around our most pressing social and environmental problems." [3] These issues are "glocal," local problems with a global impact.

PROJECT DETAILS

DESIGNS Murals
DATE July 5 to August 27, 2010
LOCATION Los Angeles, California
LEADERS Rick Valicenti and John Pobojewski (Moving Design)
DESIGNER Nick Adam
PARTNER Sixteen attendees of the Moving Design workshop
WEBSITE www.itsourwater.org, http://at.movingdesign.com/calltoaction

Moving Design brings together a coalition of designers and artists to work with community partners and use creative actions as a catalyst for change. The Call to Action, a Moving Design Intervention on Water, started with a conference about Chicago's water policy at Archeworks Studio, a multidisciplinary nonprofit design organization. [4] This Moving Design event featured twenty inspirational and informative speakers, including Bruce Mau, Clare Lyster, John Beilenberg, Daniel Eatock, Elliott Earls, Robyn Waxman, and leaders from scientific, environmental, and legislative organizations, who spoke about the water policies

Previous spread
Adam scrubs letters onto the cement walls with a deck brush and soapy water.

Opposite
Paper and Paste, poster by Scott Reinhart

Top
Downtown Data, projections by Matt Wizinsky

Bottom
Ice Craft, frozen messages by Matthew Hoffman, Rick Valicenti, Julie Heyduk, Bill Lineman, Tinne Van Loon, and Nick Adam

that control the Great Lakes and Chicago's sewer system. These lectures motivated the group to "intercept water on its way out of town and create messages that embody water: cleansing, freezing, melting, evaporations," explains Pobojewski. Artist Lisa Korpan, for example, created words out of ice cubes that sat on the ground and melted into a nearby drain, while artist Matt Wizinsky reached a different sector of Chicago's population by projecting facts about the water problem in highly trafficked public places. The group also produced posters and videos, and the workshop concluded with a parade of all participants along Michigan Avenue to the Oak Street beach.

"The credit for each idea falls on all of our shoulders, since all ideas grew through an open sourcing technique," explains graphic designer Nick Adam. "Rick Valicenti defined this process as 'rounding up': adopting or adding to another's idea and growing it to maximum potential. We developed several ideas that used water as a physical element in the messaging. All of our ideas were developed through a system of prototyping. Every concept and thought was at minimum mocked up on paper or the computer screen. The group's enthusiasm and decision to pursue a particular route determined how much prototyping was done."

Adam's own contribution to the workshop consisted of typographic water murals that he created on some of Chicago's filthiest walls with deck brushes as writing implements and buckets of soapy water. Combining familiar dialogue with script lettering, Adam's murals transcend the capabilities of posters and billboards. "Evidence of human touch is instinctively relatable," the designer says. "It's capable of stopping people in their tracks, transferring emotion, communicating passion, and activating others to be involved."

The words for each of the murals he created were brainstormed during the workshops, where the group decided on terms that would be suitable for a multitude of public applications,

DESIGN CHALLENGE

Creating awareness about Chicago's use of water and advocating for a reversal of the Chicago River.

ENGAGEMENT STRATEGY

Using a local resource, water, to emphasize the message. Consulting with water experts and design luminaries about possible approaches.

DESIGN STRATEGY

Developing ideas in teamwork. Directly integrating water into the design of the murals by using it to scrub the text onto the walls.

"Evidence of human touch is instinctively relatable. It's capable of stopping people in their tracks, transferring emotion, communicating passion, and activating others to be involved."

Nick Adam

OUTCOMES

The group gave a public face to an important issue that not many Chicago residents know about. At the end of the project, then-mayor Daley and other officials spoke about the possibility of reversing the river.

LESSONS LEARNED

Using resources that people are familiar with in ways that are tactile makes them easy to understand, relate to, and support.

such as "Drip Drop," a phrase suggested by Scott Reinhard as a metaphor for the state of water in Chicago, "Riverse Thinking," and "Da Lake." Adam also wanted to draw attention to the accumulated dirt on Chicago's infrastructure. "A wall that has been standing for over forty years is one of the dirtiest things I've ever encountered," he says. The designer painted the murals along heavily trafficked sidewalks and streets. "Almost every person on foot stopped and watched, and we did our best to engage them in a friendly banter about the issues, the mural, and how filthy the walls are," he recalls. The owners of Johalla Projects, a gallery in Wicker Park, took interest in the project and invited Adam to utilize their property in this lively neighborhood. For seven straight days, he painted a new mural on the gallery window that humanized Chicago's relationship with water. "I took inspiration from Stephen Powers's Love Letter project with the City of Philadelphia Mural Arts Program and used words that were common to personal relationships."[5] These included "We Can Fix Us" and "You and I Need to Talk," among others.

Through their efforts, the workshop participants gave a public face to an issue most people don't know about but which affects us all. As Adam states, "Each one of our actions can be seen as drops in a bucket. These drops cause the ripples that have led to spills outside of our 'bucket.'" To document and further promote the issue, Moving Design created an independently published book titled *Call to Action: An Intervention on Water* that can be purchased on Blurb.[6] Highlights of the campaign can be found at www.itsourwater.org, and the entire process is documented at at.movingdesign.com/calltoaction. Since the time the workshop took place, there have been larger public and political conversations surrounding Chicago's water (mis)usage. In a major example Alexi Giannoulias, Illinois State Treasurer, and then-mayor Richard Daley spoke about the possibility of reversing the Chicago River.

Keys for the City

Raising awareness for local music and
visual arts education programs through
a public display of altered pianos

In the summer of 2010 twenty-one pianos peppered the sidewalks
and squares of Lancaster, Pennsylvania, a city most associated with
the region's Amish and Mennonite communities. The pianos were
part of the Keys for the City campaign, launched by the nonprofit
organization Music for Everyone (MFE), "to foster creativity and
a sense of community among the general public and to raise
awareness for local music and visual arts education initiatives." To
bring this yearlong project to fruition, MFE partnered both with
city organizations and the Society of Design (SOD), dedicated to
multidisciplinary design education and community service.

      SOD elevated the impact of the initiative by recruiting local
designers, artists, and volunteers to reinvent the appearance of these
old, donated pianos before they were put out on the streets. Stored
in a warehouse where designers could work, the instruments were
altered in myriad ways. Each designer had a total of eighty hours and
250 dollars for materials to complete their piano. Keeping nearly all of
the instruments in one place during that time helped the organizers
keep track of the progress. "We had nothing in particular in mind
when we began this project," says Craig Welsh, the brains behind SOD.
"We really had no idea what to expect—we simply trusted that the

PROJECT DETAILS

DESIGNS Outdoor exhibit featuring twenty-one highback and spinnet pianos, sixteen-page newsprint guide to the project, website; hand lettering

DATE September 21, 2009 to October 23, 2010

LOCATION Lancaster, Pennsylvania

LEADERS Craig Welsh (Society of Design), Jennifer Baker (Mayor's Office of Special Events), John Gerdy (Music for Everyone)

DESIGNERS Seventeen local designers and design studios

PARTNERS Music for Everyone (MFE), Society of Design (SOD), City of Lancaster, Mayor's Office of Special Events (MOOSE)

WEBSITE www.keysforthecity.com

designers would bring the pianos to life in inspiring and energizing ways." And he was not disappointed.

One artist created a collage of hundreds of individual pieces for his piano, along with a series of short statements that he wrote on the sides of the keys. Viewers could find phrases such as "I think I love you" and "Chicken on a bone," if they were curious enough to hold down each key in order to read the messages. Another designer altered his instrument in a way that looked as if a grand piano had slammed into the back of an upright piano, resulting in a shared keyboard. One piano was painted in chalkboard paint and

Each designer had a total of eighty hours and 250 dollars for materials to complete their piano.

Previous spread
One of twenty-one pianos of the Keys for the City project

Opposite
The pianos were kept in a central location while they were designed.

Above
The local chapter of the American Institute of Architects built a shelter for a piano in one of the more prominent locations.

placed in a public park where children could draw on it with pieces of sidewalk chalk. Several pianos displayed the hand lettering of a local sign painter. Other examples included a piano featuring two large Plexiglass windows on the front that provided a clear view of the instrument's innards. "The really nice thing about having so many designers participate in the process is that there were so many different styles," Welsh says. "The diversity of design was reflective of the diversity of the community."

The citywide exhibit attracted a broad range of curious pedestrians and city dwellers who took turns playing on the pianos. A sixteen-page tabloid newsprint stated all of the piano locations and included a list of performances that would happen throughout the summer in support of the city's "Music Friday" program, which features live music in Lancaster's shops, restaurants, and city parks every third Friday of the month. Children banged out cacophonous notes, adults worked through songs they had learned when they were young, and many skilled pianists filled the streets with nostalgic melodies.

Keys for the City required nearly eight months of planning before the pianos hit the streets in mid-May 2010. The piano designs had to pass safety standards set by the city's Public Art Manager, and MFE had to fill out insurance permits and legal documents before it could place the instruments. A custom-designed bracket system had to be made to secure the pianos to the sidewalks. Finding the right locations for the instruments was another concern. "Part of the site considerations included finding some amount of coverage from rain, such as awnings, overhangs, and porticos," Welsh explains, "but several locations offered no protection, so we created custom tarps that were secured to the backs of the pianos in drawstring bags." About twenty members of the American Institute of Architects Central Pennsylvania designed, funded, and constructed a shelter for one of the most prominently displayed pianos in a public park.

DESIGN CHALLENGE
Raising awareness and money for Music for Everyone, a nonprofit organization that promotes music education.

ENGAGEMENT STRATEGY
Building partnerships with likeminded civic and municipal organizations. Utilizing free, local resources in the form of pianos and recruiting local, creative talent to design the instruments.

DESIGN STRATEGY
Giving designers and artists eighty hours and 250 dollars to transform each piano. Using imagery from the design of those pianos as source material to promote Keys for the City, Music for Everyone, and Music Friday.

"We really had no idea what
to expect—we simply
trusted that the designers
would bring the pianos
to life in inspiring
and energizing ways."
Craig Welsh

OUTCOMES

The event raised forty thousand
dollars for Music for Everyone,
business improved (especially
during Music Fridays), thousands
of people played the pianos, and
the project brought together
many different kinds of people.

LESSONS LEARNED

This large-scale project could
only be completed with the help
of many volunteers over a long
period of time. The team learned
that it takes many committed
people to bring this kind of event
to fruition.

Opposite, top
Promotional billboard

Opposite, bottom
A piano in use

Above
One of the pianos in location

Below, left
Spread from the promotional tabloid newspaper

Below, right
Music Friday in downtown Lancaster

A big question was whether the public would take care of the pianos. Would passersby cover them with the tarps if it started raining? Would the pianos be vandalized? Would people mind the sound of pianos being played late at night? "Our intention was to add to the city's cultural energy, and we hoped that the project's neighbors and community members would have a sense of ownership," Welsh says. Overall Keys for the City was widely accepted, even though one piano was covered with graffiti less than a week after being installed and another was completely destroyed, "as if someone had run into it with a truck," as Welsh describes it. One instrument had to be moved because of complaints from a resident who had difficulty sleeping when late-night passersby decided to play the piano below her window.

Charting the long-term impact of this initiative will take time, but several positive outcomes are obvious. Thousands of people have played the pianos, businesses in nearby locations enjoyed a boost, and dozens of local musicians, artists, designers, architects, and city officials collaborated in ways that rarely happen. Most importantly the community helped raise forty thousand dollars that will be used to promote important design initiatives and will provide thousands of students with better music education throughout Central Pennsylvania.

"It was a massive undertaking that required incredible generosity and commitment from many, many people and organizations," Welsh says. "It strikes me as the kind of project that while replicable probably shouldn't be. There's something magical about the project finding its way into people's lives for a short period of time and then quietly drifting along." Even so, MFE produced a smaller-scale version of the project in the summer of 2011.

Design with the Community's Voice

The style of a community may be significantly different from your personal design aesthetic. While the community may need your fresh perspective in order to break from the past, your design also needs to connect to the style of your target audience in some way.

Sample the colors, typefaces, and other style elements you come across in the community. Feature quotes, video, or audio recordings from your conversations with community members. Consider the local languages, cultural norms, and literacy levels, and continue to home in on the final design by soliciting feedback from community members throughout the design process.

If the community is diverse, you may need to create a more general entry point into the design solution. As Cavaye puts it in his essay on governance and community engagement, "Community engagement may often involve tailormade 'solutions' in different communities."[1] Welcome the opportunity of designing for a specific audience. As Canniffe pointed out in a 2008 interview, "The design solution or the design's visual language is secondary—it's informed by the community. There's this great sense of release that comes with that approach: It's not important what it looks like as much as how it changes behavior, or how it can give a voice to a community. Who really cares what it looks like, as long as the community engages with it and feels a sense of ownership—that's what's important."[2]

In this sense, community engagement requires "cultural appropriateness."[3] Let your final design mirror the voice and style of the community rather than your own to ensure that it speaks to community members and portrays the community to the world in a convincing and authentic way.

Finding the right voice for their specific audiences was a central consideration for the designers of the following two projects, Vendor Power! and The 1% User Manual.

Vendor Power!

Empowering New York City's street vendors with a brochure that translates and simplifies complex laws for many language groups

As our population grows, so does the complexity of our cities, which host millions of people and miles of infrastructure. A staggering amount of regulation exists to manage city life. Much of this policy is designed and enacted with the best intentions: to create a safer city, to make services more accessible, and to help people in need. However, the language of the law is full of jargon. Loopholes can negate a policy meant to protect; a policy can be unenforced or enforced too harshly; or its implementation can be discriminatory. In 2004 then–New York City consumer affairs commissioner Gretchen Dykstra compared the complicated set of policies regulating street vendors to an onion: "It has many layers and, after a while, one can't help but cry."[1] When people do not understand public policy, the result can be the opposite of its intent, and the underlying social needs are obscured.

The Center for Urban Pedagogy (CUP) has been working to clarify urban problems since 1997. The Brooklyn-based nonprofit organization "brings together art and design professionals with community-based advocates and researchers to make the city, its policies, processes, and infrastructure more legible so that

PROJECT DETAILS

DESIGNS A brochure that unfolds into a poster
DATE September 21, 2009 to October 23, 2010
LOCATION New York City
LEADERS Christine Gaspar, John Mangin, and Rosten Woo (Center for Urban Pedagogy); Sean Basinski (Street Vendor Project)
DESIGNER Candy Chang
PARTNER Street Vendor Project
WEBSITE www.makingpolicypublic.net

historically underrepresented groups can better participate in shaping the places where they live." It fosters collaborations that create new opportunities for designers to engage important social issues. One such series of collaborations, Making Policy Public, started in 2008 and grew out of a realization that a lot of community groups struggle to convey complex policy messages to their constituents, on whose lives the information can have a major impact.

To start these projects CUP sends out an open call to advocacy groups encouraging them to propose a convoluted public policy that needs clarification. In the past, these policies have included globalized shipping, social security, predatory equity, and the juvenile justice system, among others. A panel of four judges with a background in art, design, and advocacy chooses four of the entries. The winning policy briefs are then

In 2004 then–New York city consumer affairs commissioner Gretchen Dykstra compared the complicated set of policies regulating street vendors to an onion: "It has many layers and, after a while, one can't help but cry."

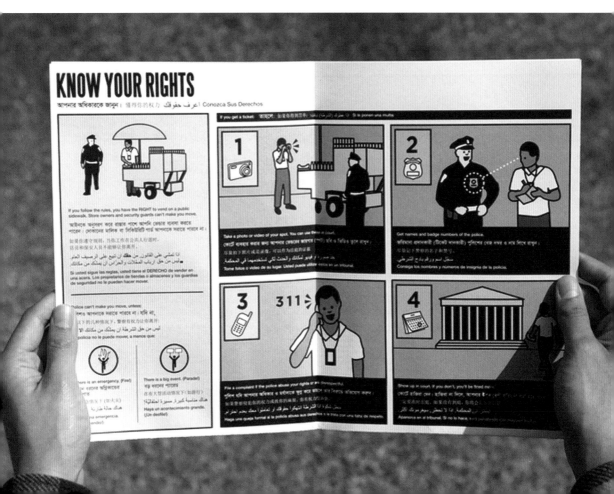

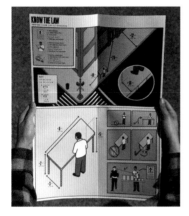

Previous spread
Street vendors use the Vendor Power! brochure as a reference.

Opposite and above
The 8.5-by-11-inch brochure unfolds into a 22-by-34-inch poster.

Top
Sean Basinski looks through a box of violation tickets that vendors received.

posted on CUP's website, and designers and artists are invited to apply to design a publication on one of them.

During the design process the designers and leaders of the advocacy group work together. CUP encourages everyone in the team to keep talking to each other throughout the six-month-long project. The advocacy group also elicits feedback from its constituency at various stages to ensure that the publication will reach those who it is designed to help. "We ask the designers to really engage the content, and the advocacy groups to really engage in the design conversation," CUP's Christine Gaspar explains.

One of the center's Making Policy Public projects is Vendor Power!, which explains New York City's complex vending regulations, educating street vendors about their rights and existing rules. The topic was proposed by the Street Vendor Project, a legal advocacy group for New York City street vendors that was started in 2001 by Sean Basinski, a lawyer and former street vendor. The organization's more than seven hundred members work together to raise public awareness about vendor issues, file lawsuits to support vendor rights, and help vendors grow their businesses by linking them with organizations providing loans and training for small businesses. Basinski was teamed up with Candy Chang, a graphic designer, and two CUP staff members, John Mangin and Rosten Woo, CUP's director at the time.

During one of the team's first meetings, Basinski showed the group a box of pink violation tickets that local vendors receive for carts that are located too close to curbs, crosswalks, and building doors; for not wearing their vending license; and for setting up on restricted streets.[2] Vendors are harshly penalized under New York City's so-called quality of life crackdowns with one thousand dollar fines. "All these regulations are buried in documents full of intimidating jargon and heinous text formatting that would make even the most patient person cry," writes Chang in an article on the Architectural League's website Urban Omnibus.[3] Over 80 percent of

DESIGN CHALLENGE

Simplifying New York City's complex vending policies for street vendors.

ENGAGEMENT STRATEGY

Partnering with the Street Vendor Project to elicit feedback from the community and to gain a thorough understanding of street vendors' needs.

DESIGN STRATEGY

Using simple graphics and illustrations that communicate across language groups and ethnicities. Translating the text into several languages so that the majority of street vendors can read it.

"Jerry Seinfeld was once a vendor, and Bloomingdale's, D'Agostino, and Macy's all started as pushcarts."

Candy Chang

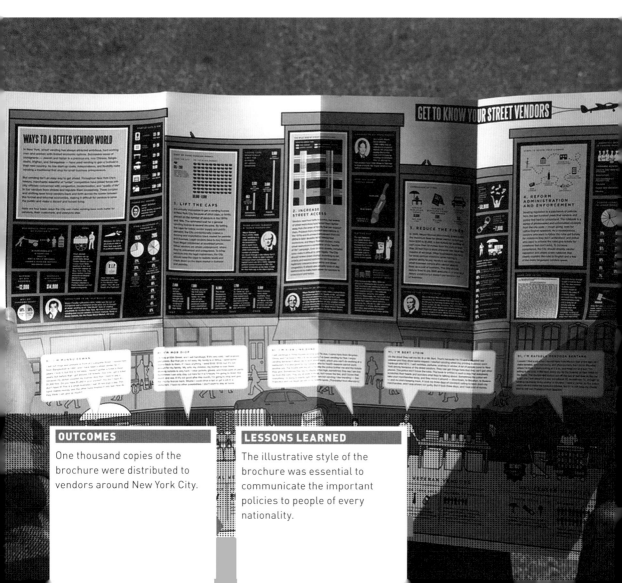

OUTCOMES

One thousand copies of the brochure were distributed to vendors around New York City.

LESSONS LEARNED

The illustrative style of the brochure was essential to communicate the important policies to people of every nationality.

vendors in Lower Manhattan are immigrants, for whom English is a second language, making these rules especially cryptic. Vending is an ideal first job for immigrants, since it comes with low start-up costs, independence, and flexibility. However, city officials frequently create new obstacles for vendors to navigate, and current caps on the number of vendors mean that getting a vending license can take several decades.

After the team established the general scope of the content, Chang created several mockups of the layout. All of the Making Policy Public publications unfold from 8.5-by-11-inch brochures into 22-by-34-inch posters. The team decided to place vendor-targeted information in the first folds, so vendors can easily access it on a day-to-day basis. "The fully opened poster was devoted to a few additional elements, including personal stories from local vendors, historical background (New York City vending started when four Jewish peddlers set up pushcarts along Hester Street), fun facts (Jerry Seinfeld was once a vendor, and Bloomingdale's, D'Agostino, and Macy's all started as pushcarts), and recommended regulation reforms (lift the license caps, increase street access, reduce the fines, and reform administration and enforcement)," explains Chang, who kept the design as pictorial as possible to communicate across languages and cultures, and included text translations in Bengali, Chinese, Arabic, and Spanish.[4]

After trying out various visual styles, the designer "eventually landed on a friendly Chris Ware–inspired style and had good times illustrating everything from hot dog stands to former mayor Ed Koch," as she recalls. [5] Feedback from vendors about the brochure's clarity, content, symbols, language, and text translations helped refine the design, which, despite being easy to understand and welcoming, has a sense of authority so that vendors can use it when dealing with police officers.

After the publication was printed, CUP organized a citywide distribution event with the help of twenty volunteers who handed out free copies of the brochure to vendors throughout the city. "Cheikh Fall, a vendor himself, helped the team map the city's vendor-dense areas and estimate numbers," John Mangin of CPU explains. "We put the posters in the hands of about one thousand vendors and received reactions ranging from enthusiastic to 'what-took-you-so-long?'"[6]

Opposite
Vendor profiles fill the inside of Vendor Power!, along with four detailed legislative changes that could improve the lives of vendors

Above and opposite top
Street vendors reading the brochure

The 1% User Manual

Encouraging architects and nonprofit organizations to collaborate

There are over 1.6 million nonprofit organizations in the United States,[1] and many of them deliver critical social services to communities in need. Most of these organizations struggle through the cycles of grant writing and fundraising, and many do not think about building strategic collaborations with architects and designers to strengthen their organizations. Nonprofit organizations "tend to see design as cosmetic and/or a luxury," says Jeremy Mende of MendeDesign. "Likewise, architecture firms often take on pro bono work, but it is usually not part of a thoughtful corporate strategy."

　　MendeDesign's *The 1% User Manual*, winner of a Sappi Ideas That Matter grant in 2006, sought to change these perceptions. The 1%, created by Public Architecture, a nonprofit organization based in San Francisco that "puts the resources of architecture in the service of public interest," is a program that connects nonprofit organizations in need of design assistance with architects willing to pledge 1 percent of their billable hours to pro bono work.

ARCHI-TECT, may we have a moment of your time?

NON-PROFIT, may we give you a moment of our time?

ISBN 978-1-60402-045-8

ISBN 978-1-60402-045-8

PROJECT DETAILS

DESIGNS Booklet; typeface: Helvetica Neue
DATE 2006
LOCATION San Francisco, California
LEADERS Jeremy Mende (MendeDesign)
DESIGNER Jeremy Mende, Stephen Knodel, Amadeo DeSousa (MendeDesign)
PARTNER Public Architecture
WEBSITE www.theonepercent.org

MendeDesign's goal with the manual was to educate nonprofits about the positive impact that design can have on an organization's effectiveness and larger brand awareness, and to remind architects that their expertise can enhance the nonprofit sector while emphasizing the benefits of having a deliberate and codified approach to pro bono work within a design studio. Mende saw the project as a great opportunity to provide a service to every nonprofit organization in the country and to widely communicate how design—architectural, graphic, interior, and environmental—can be mobilized to make the entire sector stronger and more able to meet the demands of its respective missions. "Design can be used to effectively communicate the respective stories and relevance of nonprofits. Most of their funding and resource problems come from a lack of expertise in

"It is our experience that a reader must do some of the work and be motivated to develop their own conclusions, for the work to be meaningful."

Jeremy Mende

PUBLIC ARCHITECTURE
PUTS THE RESOURCES OF ARCHITECTURE IN THE SERVICE OF THE PUBLIC INTEREST. WE IDENTIFY AND SOLVE PRACTICAL PROBLEMS OF HUMAN INTERACTION IN THE BUILT ENVIRONMENT AND ACT AS A CATALYST FOR PUBLIC DISCOURSE THROUGH EDUCATION, ADVOCACY AND THE DESIGN OF PUBLIC SPACES AND AMENITIES. 1211 FOLSOM STREET, 4TH FLOOR, SAN FRANCISCO, CA 94103-3816 T 415.861.8200 F 415.431.9695 WWW.PUBLICARCHITECTURE.ORG

telling their stories, and further, knowing what consultants to seek out in order to do this in a compelling manner," Mende explains.

MendeDesign's process is "both strategic and intuitive.... We think and we make. Through experience we know that we make the most progress by making things, testing them, discussing them, and really trying to listen to the feedback—which is sometimes hard. Often we only realize where the heart of the project is after we've taken a couple of different approaches and then—through open critique—we gain a much clearer idea of what it is we are actually trying to do." The designers started the project by interviewing Public Architecture staff members, nonprofit administrators, and architects, gathering information and beginning to develop a message hierarchy and tone that would speak to both nonprofit administrators and architects. Mende and his partners steered clear from a formally expressive, mannered aesthetic, developing a minimal approach that used an aspirational tone within an oblique, open-ended narrative. As Mende puts it, "We want to reward our audience's efforts in interacting with our work, so we always want to include enough ambiguity for the final meaning to remain open to interpretation. It is our experience that a reader must do some of the work and be motivated to develop their own conclusions, for the work to be meaningful."

MendeDesign spent eight months conceptualizing, writing, and designing *The 1% User Manual*, which consists of two volumes bound together inversely. One book is written for architects, while the other targets nonprofit administrators. Rather than incorporating imagery from both sectors, MendeDesign staff focused on writing flexible copy about The 1%, designing the manual in a way that encourages both architects and nonprofit organizations to interact with it. The shared binding serves as a metaphor for the mutually beneficial relationship that the manual is working to forge between architects and nonprofit organizations. Each book

Previous spread
Front cover of the manual

Opposite and below
MendeDesign also created a new visual identity for Public Architecture, along with a logo for The 1% program.

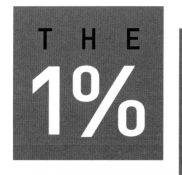

DESIGN CHALLENGE
Communicating Public Architecture's message in a booklet that speaks to both architects and nonprofit organizations.

ENGAGEMENT STRATEGY
Interviewing Public Architecture staff members, nonprofit administrators, and architects to target the design to its audience.

DESIGN STRATEGY
Developing an open-ended narrative, whose tone addresses both architects and nonprofits. Creating a booklet that encourages the reader to interact with it.

Since the publication of the manual, the number of architecture firms that have pledged to work with nonprofits has dramatically increased.

Pro bono service is vital to the health of our communities, yet it is often seen as a one-way street.

Approached strategically, it can benefit your firm in the following five ways.

>01. Creative Opportunities

>02. Recruitment & Retention

>03. Local Involvement

>04. Community Relations

>05. Personal Satisfaction

OUTCOMES

The booklet drives traffic to The 1% website. After its publication, Public Architecture's membership jumped from eighty to five hundred firms.

LESSONS LEARNED

MendeDesign learned that having complete control of the content also means a lot more content development than a small firm can easily handle.

Opposite
Architects can benefit in many ways from working pro bono for a nonprofit organization, as this spread argues.

Above
The designers utilized statistics to compel architects to donate their time and services to nonprofit organizations.

Below
Center spread of the booklet, mirroring the front cover

begins with a series of simple questions, making an emotional appeal to the respective audience group. This simple fill-in-the-blank format immediately captures the reader's attention with its interactive nature and proved to be one of the big successes of the piece. Each volume presents five specific benefits that pro bono relationships offer and outlines a best-practices model to ensure working relationships are productive and sustainable. Ultimately the booklet drives traffic to The 1% website, where architects can be paired with nonprofit groups in need of design assistance.

The project proved to be challenging. Along with winning the prestigious Sappi grant came complete control of the content, which in turn meant doing far more content development than the firm usually does. "The control allowed us to drive the design process but it was a huge amount of work for a small studio," says Mende. The results of *The 1% User Manual* are commendable. Since its launch, the number of architecture firms that have pledged to work with nonprofits has dramatically increased. Before the manual was published, Public Architecture had a membership of eighty firms. Six months after the brochure was distributed by Public Architecture, its membership had jumped to five hundred firms, and their numbers continue to grow.

Give Communities Ownership

A familiar maxim by Lao Tzu states: "Give a man a fish, feed him for a day. Teach a man to fish, feed him for a lifetime." The communities you work with will benefit from being part of the design process, and your engagement with them should include finding ways to give them ownership of tools that can continually empower them.

Show community members the various steps that are integral to the design process—which can be followed to set up something as simple as a well-run lemonade stand—such as setting goals, researching, prototyping, testing, and implementing. While they may be familiar with some of these steps, demonstrating that they are a part of a system will help community members avoid rash solutions in the future.

Foster collaborative relationships with community members in all phases of the design process. Designs that are driven by their insights and experiences will ensure that they will take ownership of it. As Cavaye points out, engagement involves balancing "the provision of resources and expertise with the importance of maintaining genuine community ownership and self reliance."[1] Look for ways to give your final design a form that can be easily duplicated or implemented so the community can add or modify the design on their own.

The designers of the following two projects, Pecans! and Hawthorne Community Center, provided communities not only with a design they could use now but with tools they could use in the future.

Pecans!

Teaching teenagers how to build a business with a plentiful local resource

Greensboro, Alabama, has become a hotspot for graphic designers around the country, who come to this town of 2,700, with a poverty rate of nearly 30 percent, to offer their design skills to help empower its population.[1,2] In January 2010 PieLab designers Robin Mooty and Amanda Buck led one such initiative, partnering with the YouthBuild Greensboro program to help underserved students create a small business using one of Alabama's most abundant resources: pecans.

YouthBuild Greensboro, established in 2006 to help the out-of-school, at-risk youth in Hale County work toward their GEDs, gain construction and hospitality training, and develop leadership skills, is one of 273 YouthBuild programs in forty-five states, Washington, D.C., and the Virgin Islands. While Youthbuild is a national organization, the Greensboro branch is operated by HERO (Hale Empowerment and Revitalization Organization), an umbrella nonprofit organization that coordinates the efforts of several nonprofits in Hale County, including Habitat for Humanity.

Mooty and Buck wanted to assist the fifteen local YouthBuild students in developing a business plan, while teaching them how to brand, market, and sell their pecan products. The

PROJECT DETAILS

DESIGNS Packaging design for eight-ounce jars of pecan butter and brittle, website; typefaces: Archer and Knockout

DATE January 2010–ongoing

LOCATION Greensboro, Alabama

LEADERS Robin Mooty and Amanda Buck (PieLab)

DESIGNERS Robin Mooty, Amanda Buck, Megan Deal, Dan Gavin, Breanne Kostyk (PieLab); fifteeen YouthBuild students

PARTNER HERO (Hale Empowerment and Revitalization Organization), YouthBuild Greensboro, Design Ignites Change

WEBSITE http://pecansproject.com

students decided to focus on pecan brittle and pecan butter, inspired by the possibility of selling their products at PieLab, a pie shop and design studio, where young designers such as Mooty and Buck work together with locals to make an impact on the Greensboro community.

During the course of the project, Mooty and Buck relied on the guidance of YouthBuild Program Director Sara Williamson and on the financial support of Design Ignites Change, an initiative run by Worldstudio and the Adobe Foundation that "supports designers and architects who want to make a difference." [3] They cowrote a proposal with other designers at PieLab and HERO and were awarded a twelve-thousand-dollar grant, which funded the business's start-up costs for six months of production supplies, including twelve hundred eight-ounce jars.

The designers included the students in every step of the process, from creative brainstorming during design workshops to codesigning and producing hundreds of labels and tags for the pecan products. "It was challenging to explain abstract concepts and processes to the students on the computer, and we found the best way to get them involved was to physically make something together," Buck and Mooty say. "We probably spent only 30 percent of our time together designing. The rest was spent cooking, baking, and canning, as well as business and financial record keeping, and creating a sustainability plan." Really getting to know the students became a key part of the project. "One of the

Mooty and Buck assisted the fifteen local YouthBuild students in developing a business plan, while teaching them how to brand, market, and sell their pecan products.

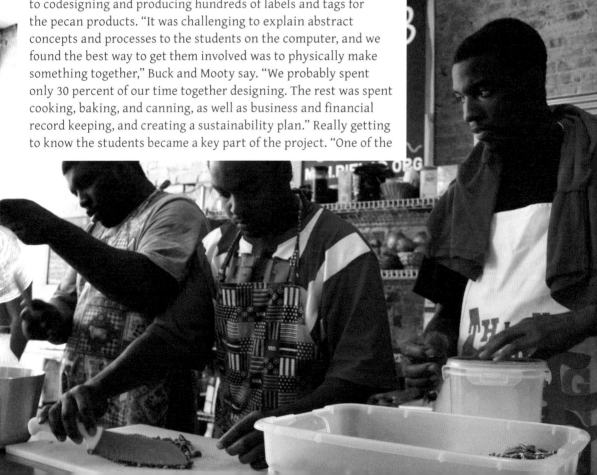

Previous spread
The finished jar of pecan butter

Opposite
Buck and Mooty involved the students in every part of the project, including making the pecan products.

Top
Buck and Mooty taught the students how to screenprint as part of the project.

Bottom
The students contributed hand-drawn logo idea sketches.

main things we learned was that design is about people," Buck and Mooty explain. "Design should improve people's lives, bring people together, and communicate messages that people understand, relate to, and respond to."

This process was not always smooth. "One of the big problems we faced was finding a creative way to motivate the students," the designers admit. "They generally showed up ready to work, but their attention spans would rarely last more than a few minutes, and it was difficult to appear as an authority figure since we weren't much older." However, the students were proud of working on a business of their own, and the Greensboro community supported the project. "The local paper let us advertise our need for pecans, and loads of people dropped off pecans from their yards. The local 'pecan guy' had a large-scale pecan cracker and cracked our pecans for free, and stores in the area agreed to sell the products," Buck and Mooty state. "People were eager to help, since we already had relationships with them through PieLab. It all came down to people: knowing people, investing in relationships, putting people first, not design."

The group set up taste-testing stands at boutique food stores in nearby Birmingham and Tuscaloosa. "This empowered the students to see people respond positively to their products," the designers recall. "Their faces would light up when they were asked to explain the process or the ingredients to tasters." This hands-on experience resulted in two perfected recipes for pecan brittle and butter. Buck and Mooty decided to produce the packaging by hand in order to give the students ownership of the design. They asked them to draw the word *pecans* over and over again, and then created a pattern with the hand lettering, which the students screenprinted on a piece of canvas. The final design of the two-by-three-inch product tag was three-layered, with the pecan pattern in the middle layer, the words *Brittle!* or *Butter!* on the top layer, and an informational, ink-jet-printed piece of colored paper

DESIGN CHALLENGE
Teaching students how to develop a business plan for their pecan products, and how to brand, market, and sell them.

ENGAGEMENT STRATEGY
Locating local, free resources to make a product that can be marketed and sold. Empowering students with skills that can help them gain control of their own career and future.

DESIGN STRATEGY
Involving the students in every part of the design process, from brainstorming ideas to screenprinting labels.

"It was challenging to explain abstract concepts and processes to the students on the computer, and we found the best way to get them involved was to physically make something together."

Amanda Buck and Robin Mooty

PECAN BRITTLE!

Made by
YouthBuild & PieLab
in Greensboro, AL

INGREDIENTS: Alabama Pecans, Sugar, Light Corn Syrup, Salt, Water, Butter, & Baking Soda.

OUTCOMES

Students learned how to start a business and how to manage it day-to-day. The pecan products are currently available for purchase online and in select stores in Alabama.

LESSONS LEARNED

Buck and Mooty learned the importance of letting go of their personal aesthetics to make something that best serves the community.

Opposite, top
The packaged brittle product

Opposite, bottom
Screenprinted tags stating the ingredients and other details accompanied each jar.

Top
Each jar of pecan brittle and butter comes with a leather strap around the lid that is branded with the word *good*.

Bottom
The pecan products were sampled by the public at a few food stores in and around Greensboro.

as the bottom layer. The designers chose Hoefler & Frere-Jones's Knockout as the typeface because "It felt like it conveyed the right amount of confidence and enthusiasm when set in all caps with an exclamation point. It contrasted well with the collagey feel of the pecans pattern of the students' drawings." Hoefler & Frere-Jones's Archer typeface, as a softer complement to Knockout, was used to set the informational text.

A leather strap, stamped with the word *good* in a Southern-style font and made by the local leathersmith, holds the tag to the jar. The strap fits snugly around the lid of the jar and doubles as a bracelet. "Our hope was that the packaging would be somehow reusable and not just thrown away. Customers get a positive souvenir with their food," the designers explain. After beginning production, Buck and Mooty realized that customers removed these tags immediately after purchasing the jars, so they added a sticker to the bottom of the jars with all of the FDA-required information.[4] The designers also created a simple website based on the elements used for the packaging design to allow the students to sell their products online. Profits from the sales of the pecan products go to the YouthBuild scholarship fund.

"What we learned in school was really only a small percentage of what we did in Greensboro," Buck and Mooty say. "We learned to design *with*, not *for*, the students, and a lot of times this meant letting go of our personal aesthetics to make something that served their purpose." The students participating in the project learned how to start a business utilizing a local resource, how to manage it day-to-day, how to market their products online and throughout the country, and ultimately, how to gain control of their own career and future. Since Buck and Mooty's involvement, a new class of YouthBuild students has created a second version of the packaging and website. Empowering Hale County's youth will lead to further empowerment for generations to come, which in turn will contribute to Greensboro's prosperity.

Hawthorne Community Center

Designing blueprints for a more effective community center

The strength of a community center relies on its ability to provide meaningful services to its clients: job seekers who need to develop new skills or learn a new language, senior citizens who want to socialize, parents who need daycare for their children. A group of graduate design students at the Herron School of Art and Design in Indianapolis spent nine months researching and proposing ways to improve the effectiveness of programs such as these for the Hawthorne Community Center, located just to the west of Indianapolis.

The center has existed for over eighty years, providing services that meet the economic, educational, social, civic, and recreational needs of the entire Hawthorne community. The students each chose to work with one of Hawthorne's several programs: English-as-a-second-language teaching, job training, after-school activities, childcare for the working poor, homeless prevention, and senior citizen services.

The project started with a tour of the community center with staff member Caleb Sutton. "Simply seeing the space helped us appreciate the gravity of the situation," says student Brian

PROJECT DETAILS

DESIGNS Proposals for various community programs; typefaces: Chaparral Pro and News Gothic

DATE September 2009 to May 2010

LOCATION Indianapolis, Indiana

LEADERS Youngbok Hong, Adrienne Dye (Herron School of Art and Design)

DESIGNERS Eleven graduate students (Herron School of Art and Design)

PARTNER Hawthorne Community Center

WEBSITE http://cargocollective.com/designthink#555040/H-A-W-T-H-O-R-N-E-C-E-N-T-E-R

Crain. "The center does not enjoy much luxury, but it buzzes with activities and classes. People were not waiting for a handout." The tour kicked off an open-ended process that had no pre-defined goals other than to empower members of the Hawthorne community. The students used participatory design research methods to understand the experiences of the center's clients and to gain insights that would guide their proposals. Their goal was to incorporate stakeholders in all phases of the design process. "Our course approached design research from a people-centered perspective," explains Crain. "We believe our clients are the experts who can best articulate their own experiences."

The students developed research tools that would help them start conversations with community members, collect data, and identify what the community needed. These tools tended to be visual in order to overcome language barriers, and many

> "Our course approached design research from a people-centered perspective," explains Crain. "We believe our clients are the experts who can best articulate their own experiences."

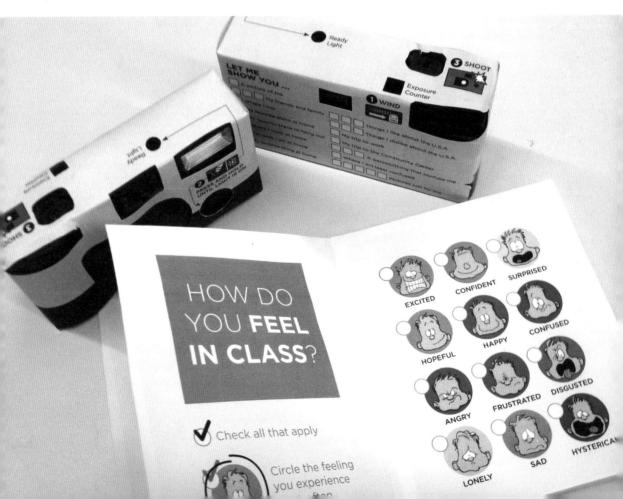

Previous spread
The students summarized their
recommendations in a large binder.

Opposite and this page, bottom
As part of the team's research, children
were given disposable cameras with a list of
categories suggesting subjects for photos.

Top
The design team spent a lot of time analyzing
the responses and feedback from the
Hawthorne groups.

of them served as cultural probes that were sent home with the
participants to document their lives. For example, the children in
the childcare for the working poor group were given disposable
cameras with a list of suggested topics for photographs printed
on the camera case, such as "Where I live" or "My friends and
family." Participants also used workbooks to draw their families
and describe their feelings. Other tools were generative, consisting
of activities that the students did together with the participants
at the center, such as making collages that could be used as
visual prompts during the design process. However, not all of the
students found these toolkits to be helpful.

"My biggest regret is not making stronger connections
with just a few key people and really getting to understand them in
a much more personal way," admits Anna d'Ambrosio, who worked
with senior citizens. "Instead, I felt pressure as a designer to make
a kit for the seniors, and then I had to practically beg them to fill it
out. I realized just how important it is to have incentives built into
everything." Classmate Brandon Stuck had similar frustrations.
"In the future I would offer enticements to participants at the
beginning of the project, rather than attempting to offer them
only after we encountered problems."

The Hawthorne community is almost entirely composed of
immigrants who were suspicious of outsiders inquiring about their
lives and experiences. "I wish the people in charge of the center
had better understood what we do before we started the project,"
says d'Ambrosio. "It taught us to articulate our goals better."
Over time, however, the students earned the trust of the families
they regularly worked with. "Nothing was better than when the
children came to know and trust me, and would come running to
greet me when I entered the center," recalls Crain.

After the initial research phase, the students analyzed
and synthesized the data into visual experience maps that helped
them identify specific problems and opportunities within their

DESIGN CHALLENGE
Researching the programs at
Hawthorne Community Center to
find out how they can be improved.

ENGAGEMENT STRATEGY
Involving community members
in the research by developing
participatory research tools.

DESIGN STRATEGY
Analyzing the feedback from
community members and
proposing improvements in a
master binder that includes
maps, diagrams, photographs,
and writing.

The proposals ranged from fourteen to eighteen pages and included a mix of photographs, illustrations, diagrams, and charts describing the respective program, the students' research, and their recommendations for improvements.

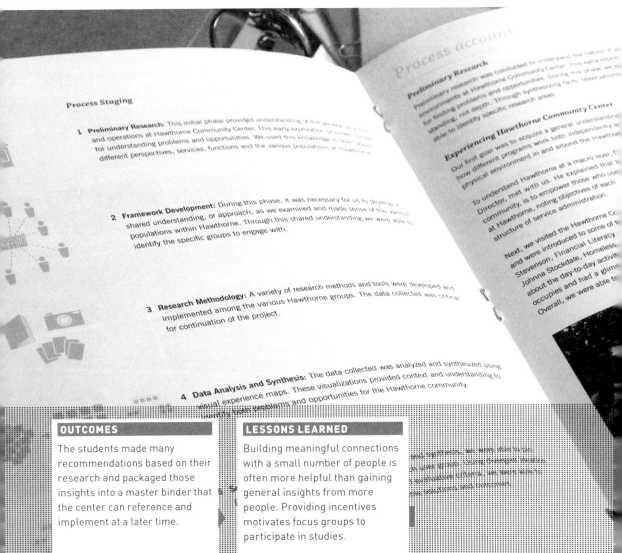

Process Staging

1 **Preliminary Research:** This initial phase provided understanding of the general structure and operations at Hawthorne Community Center. This early exploration provided the basis for understanding problems and opportunities. We used this knowledge to learn about different perspectives, services, functions and the various populations at Hawthorne.

2 **Framework Development:** During this phase, it was necessary for us to develop a shared understanding, or approach, as we examined and made sense of the various populations within Hawthorne. Through this shared understanding, we were able to identify the specific groups to engage with.

3 **Research Methodology:** A variety of research methods and tools were developed and implemented among the various Hawthorne groups. The data collected was critical for continuation of the project.

4 **Data Analysis and Synthesis:** The data collected was analyzed and synthesized using visual experience maps. These visualizations provided context and understanding to identify both problems and opportunities for the Hawthorne community.

Process account

Preliminary Research

Preliminary research was conducted to understand the nature of environments at Hawthorne Community Center. This early exploration for finding problems and opportunities. During this phase we standing, not depth. Through synthesizing facts, observations, able to identify specific research areas.

Experiencing Hawthorne Community Center

Our first goal was to acquire a general understanding how different programs work both independently a physical environment in and around the Hawthorne

To understand Hawthorne at a macro level, c Director, met with us. He explained that t community, is to empower those who use at Hawthorne, noting objectives of each structure of service administration.

Next, we visited the Hawthorne Co and were introduced to some of t Stevenson, Financial Literacy Johnna Stockdale, Homeless about the day-to-day activit occupies and had a glim Overall, we were able t

OUTCOMES

The students made many recommendations based on their research and packaged those insights into a master binder that the center can reference and implement at a later time.

LESSONS LEARNED

Building meaningful connections with a small number of people is often more helpful than gaining general insights from more people. Providing incentives motivates focus groups to participate in studies.

particular groups in the Hawthorne community. They developed a series of proposals based on these systematic and collaborative research projects, each focusing on improving a particular service at the Hawthorne Community Center. For example, they envisioned the after-school program as an opportunity to teach children about family activities that could improve their parents' English skills. Another proposal consisted of an Empowerment Toolkit that would enable directors of the homeless prevention program to work with the homeless to analyze how their choices have and will affect their living situation. The group of students who worked with senior citizens designed a new program called the Living Legacy, which aims at increasing the variety in a senior's day and their opportunities to talk about the past.[1]

The proposals ranged from fourteen to eighteen pages and included a mix of photographs, illustrations, diagrams, and charts describing the respective program, the students' research, and their recommendations for improvements. Distilling collaborative research processes into a clear directive for the future, the proposals empowered the center's primary clients to influence the shape of services offered to them.

While the administrators of the center were extremely happy with the students' research and insights, implementing their proposals will require additional funding and staff at the Hawthorne Community Center. The center is currently undergoing a capital campaign to build a new structure with additional services, and the students anticipate that their proposals will be included in these plans. Not only will Hawthorne have a new facility for the first time in over eighty years, but the center's staff will also have strategic insights to form a more thoughtful system of programs.

Opposite
The students presented their research in booklets that summarized their research approach, samples of feedback from different groups at Hawthorne, and the group's final recommendations to develop and improve the programs.

Below
Booklet focusing on Hawthorne's family program

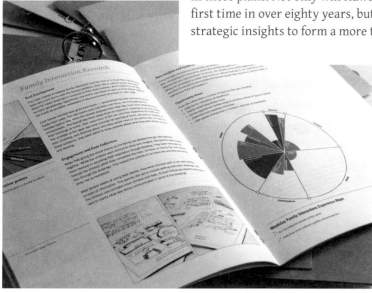

Sustained Engagement

The bonds you form with community members will be similar to those of a friendship. Solidify your partnership by working with them even after you meet the initial goals of your project. The better you get to know a community, the more you will understand its needs and how design can help.

Offer your periodic design services, start an internship or apprenticeship program with youths in the community, join the community's leadership board, or discover another way to stay in frequent contact with community leaders. Build relationships with nonprofit organizations in your own neighborhood that are based on mutual interests. Over time, your input as an invested neighbor with informed insights can lead to more effective and relevant designs.

As with all relationships, it will take time to get to this stage and it may be difficult to sustain that close connection, but your perspective as a design consultant can improve the way a community operates and support its members. The following two projects, Walk in My Shoes and One + 1, show designers who stayed committed to the communities they worked with and still have an active relationship with them today.

Walk in My Shoes

Assisting a nonprofit organization in promoting and documenting a performance by at-risk youths

Old Arizona is a haven for teenage girls in southern Minneapolis who need guidance to make positive life choices. Darcy Knight founded this large nonprofit organization in 1995 to provide a safe space for young girls who tend toward a life of crime and prostitution. Old Arizona combines art classes with mentoring and gender-specific programs at no cost to participants. The neighborhood has become much safer since Knight and her coworkers started their outreach in 1993, but the organization still needs to build awareness in order to increase community participation and fund their projects. Piece Studio recognized this need in 2010 and won a 4,250-dollar Sappi Ideas That Matter grant to assist Old Arizona in producing a performance called *Walk in My Shoes* that featured twenty-three teenage girls.

Bernard Canniffe cofounded Piece Studio, together with Mike Weikert and Oliver Munday, in 2007, with a focus on collaborative and participatory design that is broad, all-encompassing, and research-driven. "We believe in a process where everyone has an equal voice and everyone is a designer to create opportunities for people who have none," says Canniffe. The team

PROJECT DETAILS

DESIGNS Posters, tickets, programs, set design, book, video; typefaces: Gill Sans and Caslon
DATE September 2010 to March 2011
LOCATION Minneapolis, Minnesota
DESIGNERS Bernard Canniffe, J. Zachary Keenan (Piece Studio)
PARTNER Old Arizona
WEBSITE www.oldarizona.com, www.piecestudio.org

usually spends more time getting to know a community's needs and building relationships than designing. Their collaboration with Old Arizona started as an intensive twelve-week performing arts youth workshop during the summer of 2010, leading up to a performance. Initially, Piece Studio and Old Arizona planned to develop the performance together. When Old Arizona was awarded its own grant to produce *Walk in My Shoes*, the designers instead concentrated on producing the promotional materials for the show.

The students taking part in the production called themselves "Blendid Minds"—a combination of "blended" and "splendid"—and

"We make it clear what our expectations are and keep promises to ourselves and the community, but sometimes this is not enough."

Bernard Canniffe

Previous spread
Teenagers rehearse for their production, *Walk in My Shoes*.

Left
Taylor Lindgren's poster, which became the final promotional poster for the performance

Opposite
Two of Piece Studio's poster designs that Old Arizona rejected in favor of Lindgren's poster

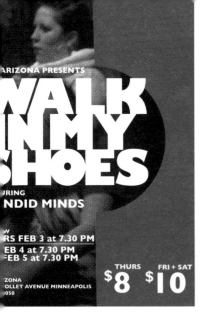

were involved in all aspects of the production, including lighting and set design, operating the board, and working together with Piece Studio to design promotional posters, tickets, and the event program. They also wrote the text of the performance, which was based on their own experiences and ambitions, and set the words to music and dance under the direction of choreographer Amy Sackett and songwriter Roosevelt Mansfield.

Canniffe and fellow Piece Studio designer J. Zachary Keenan spent a lot of time at rehearsals in order to get to know the community. "Sometimes we just watched the rehearsals but we often talked to Old Arizona's staff and the teenagers," Canniffe explains. He found it difficult to keep people's attention, which he attributed to the age difference and the large number of people involved in the project. "Rehearsals were extremely chaotic, and I think people saw us as a distraction," he says. "I feel they didn't understand why we were there, probably because we were not actively designing." Canniffe admits that even though Piece Studio has been doing community-based projects for many years, the designers are still learning how to be effective and responsive. "We make it clear what our expectations are and keep promises to ourselves and the community, but sometimes this is not enough," he says.

Throughout the design process, Canniffe and Keenan met with a large number of people, including Old Arizona staff, the song and dance coordinators, and the performers themselves. "We learned what their influences are and got their responses to some of our color, shape, and type studies," Canniffe explains. "We wanted to avoid the predictable stereotypes and clichés associated with graffiti." Featuring Gill Sans and Caslon type and a combination of script lettering laid over photographs of the teenagers, the studio's final poster design portrayed the show as if it were a Broadway performance. Decreased leading and kerning, along with text running off the poster's edges, heighten the tension in order to express the underlying themes of conflict and resolution in the performance.

DESIGN CHALLENGE

Helping an organization promote an original production with at-risk youths.

ENGAGEMENT STRATEGY

Interviewing the teenagers and Old Arizona staff to elicit feedback for the designs. Maintaining contact with Old Arizona after the end of the project by serving on the Board of Trustees.

DESIGN STRATEGY

Avoiding stereotypes and clichés in the design. Portraying the show as if it were performed on Broadway.

Left
As part of their collaboration with Old Arizona, the designers created a book that featured the teenage performers.

Below
The performers during the night of the show

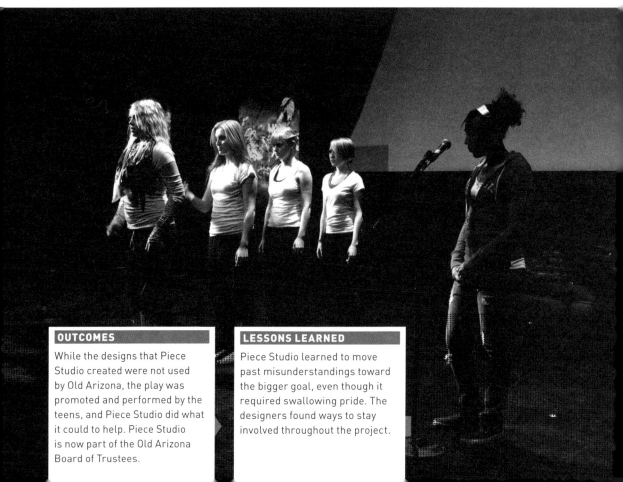

OUTCOMES

While the designs that Piece Studio created were not used by Old Arizona, the play was promoted and performed by the teens, and Piece Studio did what it could to help. Piece Studio is now part of the Old Arizona Board of Trustees.

LESSONS LEARNED

Piece Studio learned to move past misunderstandings toward the bigger goal, even though it required swallowing pride. The designers found ways to stay involved throughout the project.

When the designers presented their solution, they were surprised to learn that Blendid Minds didn't like the firm's designs and wanted to use those of a young graffiti artist—Taylor Lindgren, who had worked with Old Arizona before—instead. "We were shocked to learn that Old Arizona wanted to use Taylor's poster, tickets, and program, but this really speaks to the heart of what social design is," Canniffe admits, alluding to his belief that community-based projects are much more complex and volatile than other design projects. "They may have liked Tyler's designs because he was their age or maybe he better represented what Old Arizona stands for. It was scary, daunting, and humbling at the same time, but it was important that Old Arizona and Blendid Minds loved the designs." Many designers would have given up on working with a partner organization that did not fully disclose that it was also engaging the services of another designer, but Canniffe and Keenan swallowed their pride and continued to immerse themselves into the rehearsals and to document the process. "The design aesthetic is secondary to empowering the community," Canniffe explains. "If we are doing our job right, then the community's voice outweighs our own. It was always about them and never about Piece Studio. As designers we take our craft seriously, but it is one part of the many, where all parts are equal. What mattered is that we helped and supported Old Arizona throughout the process."

Walk in My Shoes was performed at Old Arizona in February 2011 to rave reviews from attendees. The performance was a series of vignettes, dealing with family and relationship conflicts and portraying the students' ideal world. "The teens produced a remarkable and inspirational performance," Canniffe recalls. "They learned to dance and sing, but more importantly they came to respect each other and themselves. They became a stronger community and more self-aware."

This was a special journey for Piece Studio. "It was important to move through the initial misunderstanding with ease, though it made us feel so inadequate," Canniffe says. "Maybe we were feeling that design is sometimes inadequate. Designers are only effective when we listen to the needs of everyone and humble ourselves to realize we are a small and important cog in a large matrix that is full of many important and vital constituents. I believe it is important that we think of social workers as designers, community leaders as designers, and teenagers as designers." Canniffe will continue to listen and help Old Arizona. He currently serves as a board member, bringing a design perspective to important matters as the nonprofit continues to shape its vision and programming.

"Designers are only effective when we listen to the needs of everyone and humble ourselves to realize we are a small and important cog in a large matrix that is full of many important and vital constituents."

Bernard Canniffe

One + 1

Promoting a mentoring program through
marketing and other materials

Most graphic design graduates are eager to find their first paying
design jobs, but the partners of the newly established San
Francisco–based studio Rise-and-Shine wanted more than that. In
2004 Melissa Tioleco-Cheng, Robert J. Williams, Darren Ferriera,
and Yoshie Matsumoto focused on creating positive change,
"before the world of commerce got us," as Tioleco-Cheng recalls.

They applied for a Sappi Ideas That Matter grant,
reviewing over two hundred local nonprofit organizations to find
a cause with maximum impact, a group whose mission and track
record matched their own determination "to do good—well," and
an organization that would markedly benefit from their help.
The team narrowed their choices to three, interviewed each, and
finally chose Friends for Youth, a national agency that provides
mentoring for at-risk teens, steering them away from harmful
lifestyles of crime, gangs, and drugs.

"We feel that a healthy youth population breeds a healthy
society," Tioleco-Cheng explains. "The qualities attained via
[Friends for Youth's] mentorship, such as personal stability, self-
motivation, inner peace, and feelings of interconnectedness,

are contagious and can be spread from the community outwards." Friends for Youth has been helping teens since 1979, but its communication materials were outdated and needed to be improved. Rise-and-Shine Studio wanted to support the organization by providing it with a collection of sharper, more effective tools, along with blueprints to forge more in the future.

The designers worked hard to win the Sappi grant. Their strategy was to "go above and beyond" the typical proposal, combing over the design details and proposal arguments for months and finally delivering a bound book with a mounted set of presentation boards that thoroughly explained how they would use the money. Their labor of love received praise for "raising the bar" for proposal entries at Sappi, along with the largest grant awarded that year: fifty thousand dollars.

At the beginning of the project, Tioleco-Cheng, Williams, Ferriera, and Matsumoto researched stories of former mentees who had directly benefited from the program. These gave them the idea of naming their campaign "One + 1," alluding to the fact that it takes only one person to make an exponentially positive difference in an individual's life. Friends for Youth sets this

Previous page
Rise-and-Shine designed a large number of items for Friends for Youth, including this summary of the organization's outreach program.

This page and opposite
The centerpiece of the campaign was a journal for mentees.

"The qualities attained via [Friends for Youth's] mentorship, such as personal stability, self-motivation, inner peace, and feelings of interconnectedness, are contagious and can be spread from the community outwards."

Melissa Tioleco-Cheng

process in motion by connecting two people, with numerous positive outcomes for the youth, the mentor, and society.

The Rise-and-Shine partners used this formula to promote Friends for Youth's mission to people of all language groups as well as the illiterate, making a special effort to neutralize the "victim" aspect of at-risk youths and instead emphasize the positive strengths of partnering. They avoided images that portrayed doe-eyed, needy-looking youth or shady neighborhoods in favor of those showing happy friendships and fun mentoring events, pointing to solutions.

They also made sure to balance their own design sensibilities with Friends for Youth's expertise. As Tioleco-Cheng puts it, "We had to choose our battles carefully and drop our egos to work in collaboration with our client for the sake of a better end product." For example, the Rise-and-Shine designers felt that Friends for Youth's logo was outdated. "We were afraid that it didn't hit the 'cool' mark with the teens and that they might be turned off from the program entirely," Tioleco-Cheng explains. "A short way into the redesign, we realized that Friends for Youth really loved their logo and were not interested in changing it, and that our energy was needed elsewhere." As a compromise, the designers created modern illustrations and structured layouts to balance out the hand-lettered, whimsical logo. "Working with communities always reminds us that at the end of every product is a human being, not just a user, consumer, or prospective client," Tioleco-Cheng says. "Today, we consider the art of design to heavily include the art of listening."

The studio designed a range of print materials to advance the goals of the organization. To generate interest among at-risk teens, the designers crafted a dynamic information brochure about the mentoring program and an engaging and informative keepsake mentoring journal. "Our first versions of the Weekly

DESIGN CHALLENGE

Supporting a youth-mentoring organization by improving its outdated communication tools.

ENGAGEMENT STRATEGY

Speaking with former mentees who had benefited from the program. Continuing to work with Friends for Youth after the project was completed.

DESIGN STRATEGY

Creating modern illustrations that speak to young mentees. Developing templates that Friends for Youth can use in the future to update their designs.

"Working with communities always reminds us that at the end of every product is a human being, not just a user, consumer, or prospective client."

Melissa Tioleco-Cheng

OUTCOMES

The One + 1 campaign improved Friends for Youth's public image and reputation, while successfully soliciting donations, youth referrals, parental support, and volunteer mentors. The mentoring journal is still in use five years later.

LESSONS LEARNED

The designers learned the importance of letting go of ego when working with a community and to be open to compromises.

Opposite, top
Every mentee must have his or her parents
or guardian sign a contract that shows
their agreement with the Friends for Youth
program.

Opposite, bottom
The designs are color-coded for streamlined
office use.

Above
The designers created exhibition booth display
cases, including this brochure holder.

Entry pages had a lot of abstract art to inspire creativity," recalls Tioleco-Cheng. "This made the pages seem untouchable to the community. And many users feel more comfortable just writing. So, subsequent reprints were revised with cleaner pages and minimal illustration." In an email to the designers, Michael J. Karcher, coeditor of the *Handbook of Youth Mentoring*, calls Rise-and-Shine Studio's mentoring journal "the most sophisticated and creative tool I've seen for structuring and documenting the life of a match. When fully utilized by mentors, the mentoring journal appears to provide a flexible, fun, and engaging mentoring activity, especially for older teens with whom it can be quite difficult to establish a connection."

The designers also created an annual report that was full of hard numbers and a lot of heart to persuade donors, a new mail-ready brochure directed at volunteers, and a bilingual brochure for Spanish-speaking parents and high school students. The complete collateral system tells a clear and consistent story. It is image-heavy to provide a quick read to people from a range of ages and cultures and thoughtfully colored to produce a sense of grounded optimism. The pieces were designed according to their content and audience, but also for ease of use. The brochures are mail-ready individually or can be combined in any combination into a marketing folder; each is color-coded and labeled along the spine for streamlined office use.

The One + 1 print campaign has strengthened Friends for Youth's image, reputation, and friendships while successfully soliciting donations, youth referrals, parental support, and volunteer mentors for the many youths stranded on the waiting list. The new materials enable the organization to communicate its mission and services more effectively, and are still being used five years later, thanks to Rise-and-Shine's commitment to working with the organization. Today the studio stays informed about Friends for Youth by maintaining a donor status that allows them to continue the relationship at specific, donor-related events and lectures.

Engagement Strategies

IMMERSE YOURSELF
+ Spend time getting to know the community you work with.
+ Regularly visit community leaders and engage them as partners throughout the design process.
+ Work side-by-side with members of the community and observe their daily lives.
+ Volunteer your time to help community members meet their needs.
+ Be prepared to give up a certain amount of control and let the community's input inform your design decisions.
+ Be clear in your communication with community partners.

BUILD TRUST
+ Find ways to bond and build strong relationships with community members.
+ Meet one of the community's basic design needs quickly.
+ Help community members in their daily operations, make a meal for them, or give them a gift.
+ Show community members that you take them seriously and truly care.

PROMISE ONLY WHAT YOU CAN DELIVER
+ Avoid trying to solve all of the community's design needs.
+ Accurately estimate the time and resources you can contribute.
+ Identify the deadline of the project and plan backwards.
+ Establish a budget and stick to it.
+ Identify assets in the community, such as established infrastructure and services or unique skills or resources, that you can build on.

PRIORITIZE PROCESS
+ Avoid quick solutions by just giving community members what they want.
+ Thoroughly research the design problem before proposing solutions.

+ Generate numerous prototypes before coming to a final, informed strategy.
+ Let community members know at the beginning of the project that you follow a process that may lead you to an unexpected solution.
+ Bring transparency to your work by explaining each step you take.

CONFRONT CONTROVERSY

+ Assess the purpose of the project and think about what message your design should convey.
+ Address controversial topics head on.
+ Make your solutions tasteful while emphasizing outcomes that the community needs.
+ Conduct focus groups with community members to gauge their reactions to the problem and use what you learned to guide your work.
+ Meet with community partners frequently to make sure that your design effectively addresses the controversial issues with taste and playfulness.

IDENTIFY THE COMMUNITY'S STRENGTHS

+ Address the community's challenges in an uplifting tone.
+ Craft your design in a way that focuses on a community's strengths.
+ Identify the unique qualities of community members as well as the challenges they face and use that list as a guide throughout the project.
+ Help community members become more confident about their role in meeting their own needs.

UTILIZE LOCAL RESOURCES

+ Find ways to build on the community's established resources.
+ Survey the community to determine what local material resources are plentiful and consider incorporating them into your design.
+ Learn what skills or talents community members can contribute during the design process.

DESIGN WITH THE COMMUNITY'S VOICE

+ Make sure your design connects to the community's style and doesn't just reflect your own aesthetics.
+ Research what colors, typefaces, and other style elements are prevalent in the community and take inspiration from them.
+ Feature quotes, video, or audio recordings from your conversations with community members in your design.
+ Consider the local languages, cultural norms, and literacy levels, and continue to home in on your final design by soliciting feedback from community members throughout the design process.

GIVE COMMUNITIES OWNERSHIP

+ Empower the community by giving it ownership over design tools and methods.
+ Involve community members from the beginning so that they can learn from the research, brainstorming, and planning phases of the project and take pride in it.
+ Choose a form for the design that can be easily duplicated and provide clear instructions along with thorough training.

SUSTAINED ENGAGEMENT

+ Solidify your partnership with the community by keeping in touch with community members after you meet the initial goals of your project.
+ Offer your periodic design services or start an internship or apprenticeship program with youths in the community.
+ Join the community's board or discover another way to stay in frequent contact with community leaders.

Funding
Social Design

Strategies to help fund small to large projects

Many of the projects featured in this book were funded by one or more grants. Others were produced by studios or students who worked pro bono. While it is often difficult for underfunded organizations to pay designers adequately, the design process requires a significant amount of time, and designers should always expect some form of compensation for their work. As IDEO's Design for Social Impact guide states, "Pro bono engagements should be an exception rather than the rule. We do better work when we are paid because we can apply the time and other resources to do an exceptional job rather than applying less experienced people in their spare time."[1]

This chapter features funding approaches that designers can use to execute community-based projects. These include tips on how to benefit from working with organizations that cannot pay you, advice from designers about the grant writing process, examples of self-initiated funding projects and community-supported microgrants, and a profile of a design nonprofit that generates its own funding. These strategies are part of a flexible and sustainable grassroots movement that utilizes our interconnectivity to meet a variety of needs. Use one of these approaches to fund your upcoming project, find ways to combine these and other strategies, or be inspired and create a new approach to fit your needs.

Youth of every age are the lifeblood of UMAR. Some are there to box, some to learn, and others just to spend time with each other. Shaikira, 13, says it perfectly:

"it is a happy thing for me to do."

PLEASE CONTINUE THE SUCCESS OF THIS PROGRAM

SUPPORT UMAR

FINANCIAL CONTRIBUTIONS MAY BE MADE TO:
UMAR Youth and Boxing, Inc.
c/o David Schorr, CPA
1217 W. North Avenue
Baltimore, Maryland 21217

or donate online at:
www.nohooksbeforebooks.org

e UMAR Youth and Boxing Program is a 501©(3) tax-exempt,
icly supported organization. It is registered with the State of
nd with the Maryland Charitable Solicitations Act.

ns to UMAR are Tax-deductible as provided in section
ernal Revenue code.

n appreciated stock are avoidable. Donate
via our Merrill Lynch brokerage account and
ns for the stock's full value.

PRO BONO WORK

Underfunded communities and organizations may not be able to locate money in their budgets for design, but they can provide you with other forms of compensation. It is usually up to the designer to point this out. For example, Zerofee, an "ethical graphic design agency" in London, will work for free if it has "reasonable creative control" and "no strict deadlines."[2] Many design studios have similar guidelines for pro bono work, but few codify them as well as Rise-and-Shine Studio. The San Francisco–based firm includes a number of clauses in its contract that stipulate alternative forms of compensation for the designers' efforts. These clauses have included:

COPYRIGHT AND CREDIT

The designer reserves the right to include a name credit and URL in a discreet position on all design materials. Websites will include a link to the designer's website for promotional purposes.

PARTICIPATION OF THE EXECUTIVE DIRECTOR

The client's executive director or top decision-maker agrees to attend design presentations. As Rise-and-Shine's Tioleco-Cheng explains, "This makes sure that the company is invested in the time we are donating and that all decisions will be made with the boss's okay—so we won't have to reroute work back to initial stages of work if, in the end, the boss does not agree with the final product."

DONOR STATUS

The organization grants the designers a donor status that is equivalent to the amount of what their design fee would be. This membership clause costs the client nothing, but emphasizes the value of design work. It also allows designers to continue their relationship with the organization by being invited to events and lectures.

BIDDING PRIVILEGES

The client will invite the designer to bid on future paying design projects for a predetermined period of time.

PERIODIC FEEDBACK

The organization agrees to respond to brief feedback questionnaires about the designs at one-, three-, and five-year increments. This feedback will give designers a tool to continually refine their process.

TESTIMONIALS

Clients agree to provide a testimonial of their experience working with the designer, which may be published by the designer for promotional purposes.[3]

There are many ways to be compensated for pro bono work. Adding clauses such as these will help you remain motivated through the difficult parts of the design process and will help your client realize the value of your efforts. Be creative and consult with community leaders to learn what they can offer you for your time and energy.

GRANT WRITING INSIGHTS

Grant applications are time-consuming. Not only do you need to propose a compelling project to work on, but you also have to submit a compelling application to the funding organization. This means translating your research into clear writing and graphics that persuade funders to grant you money. Community organizations will often have a list of grants that they applied for in the past or wanted to apply for. If the organization you partner with works on environmental or educational topics, they might apply for government grants through grants.gov. Several of the designers mentioned in this book funded their projects with Sappi Ideas That Matter grants, which are awarded once a year to designers who work with nonprofits. Some students who contributed to this book won Design Ignites Change's Implementation and Idea Awards, which are awarded by the Adobe Foundation and Worldstudio Projects.

Nonprofit and fundraising websites are filled with information and advice about applying for grants. Some even provide templates. The Center for Urban Pedagogy's Christine Gaspar recommends consulting the Foundation Center (www. foundationcenter.org) for those who are writing their first grant application. The Foundation Center proves to be a good website to search for grants as well. Its database includes details about one hundred thousand funders and nearly 2.5 million grants. While this subscription service comes at a price, it may be worth purchasing if you are serious about applying for a grant. The Foundation Center also sponsors Cooperating Collections, which are information centers in libraries throughout the country that provide information to people looking for grants.[4] Beyond the guidelines and advice from these websites and databases, keep in mind the following points from contributors to this book when you start your grant writing process.

BUILD RELATIONSHIPS WITH NONPROFITS AND FUNDING ORGANIZATIONS

It may make sense to partner with a nonprofit for your grant application. As Gaspar points out, "Most funds are not directly available to designers unless they are working in partnerships [with nonprofit organizations] or through fiscal sponsorships." Nonprofit organizations can be held accountable because, among other reasons, their tax records are public information.

Once you have established a connection with the nonprofit, Gaspar recommends getting to know the funders and meeting them personally, if possible. The likelihood of your application rising to the top of the pile may be depend on how well staff members of the funding organization know you personally and are convinced by your dedication to the cause. Tioleco-Cheng explains the various steps both processes might involve: "We research the nonprofit via annual reports, its website, on-site visits, and interviews with the staff and its benefactors. We then expand our research outwards to gain an understanding of the organization's local environment and industry. Finally, we research the grant-givers themselves and the competition in question to gain an understanding of motivation—what they are looking for. We search for information on past grant recipients, their causes/benefactors, and the final products they developed with the help of the grant."

The time this takes will depend on the complexity of your project and the expectations of the funding organization in question. Tioleco-Cheng estimates that Rise-and-Shine Studio spends between one and four months to complete a grant application, depending on the firm's familiarity with the information and how busy its designers are with other projects.

SUPPLY GOOD CONTENT

As a graphic designer with strong typography and layout skills, you have an advantage over many grant seekers who rely on templates and traditional word processing software. Tioleco-Cheng and her team at Rise-and-Shine are particular about the look of their grant applications. "Apart from the fact that it must be designed (no Word documents from us) in order to really tell the story of the cause," she says, "we understand that it also must be intelligible and easy to get through (the judges have to look through hundreds). We rely heavily on informational graphics and create [proposals] that are clean, easy to navigate, thorough, and poetic."

While designing your application will help make it stand out, the information you include about the project will always be more important than the styling that you use to talk about it. Funders will want to know how you will grow their investment into something else, how long it will take for that growth to occur, and how confident you are that growth will actually happen. These details should be summarized early on in your application in one succinct sentence: "If you provide me with [blank] amount of money or resources, then I will be able to complete [blank] project in [blank] amount of time."[5]

As Gaspar explains further, "Funders always want to know how you define success and how you will evaluate the success of your programs. They want to know who your target audience is, how you are serving them, how you are incorporating them into your process or project. They want to see a budget that is realistic and some idea of what you will do if you don't get your full grant request. Can you scale back the project? Can you start working on a piece of it? Do you have other funds? You are asking them to give you money so that you can address some issue or need in the world; they will expect you to show that the need in fact exists and how you know that it exists. If you are working in well-developed areas (education, for example), it's probably good to demonstrate that you are not re-creating the wheel and that you have some sense of how other education programs work, how they evaluate success, and so on."

Make sure you read the grant application form and submission guidelines thoroughly. BRUTE LABS's Joshua To emphasizes how important it is to tailor your submission to the funding organization's requirements and recommends repeatedly using terminology or buzzwords from the submission guidelines, letting funders know that you paid attention to their requests.

ACCURATELY ESTIMATE COSTS

Be sure to account for every calculable expense of the project, including the costs of office supplies, equipment, paper, printing, postage, conducting focus groups, food, travel, and personnel. It is usually better to list the costs for more expensive production alternatives to account for any price fluctuations. As Tioleco-Cheng explains, "If we have a mishap—such as the nonprofit delivering approval late, causing the job to require rush delivery—then we may downsize the production as needed. If we aren't required to use rush delivery, we'll opt for the better production option." Accurate budgets are the result of experience. As Gaspar states, "Every budget you do will be better than the last one. Keep good track of your costs as you work on a project, then look back when you start the next budget."

"The more compellingly you communicate your story, the more likely you are to receive support. People like to fund honest, compelling, impactful stories."

Craig Welsh

INCORPORATE STORYTELLING INTO YOUR APPLICATION

Supplement the hard facts and numbers with the human story behind the project. "The more compellingly you communicate your story, the more likely you are to receive support," advises Craig Welsh of Society of Design. "People like to fund honest, compelling, impactful stories." Tioleco-Cheng agrees, adding that "proposals need to be personal to donors, demonstrating the human need and appealing to their sense of community and good will." Tailor your story to the details of the grant application form, specifying the opportunities the grant will provide you with and using images and supporting quotes from the community you want to work with. As Ramzy Masri puts it, "People respond well to proposals that feel human and self-aware. I like to sprinkle in humor and asides as a way of breaking the fourth wall."[6]

FOLLOW UP WITH THE FUNDING ORGANIZATION

Perhaps the most commonly overlooked step of the grant-writing process is following up with the organization after you have applied. Call or email the organization to ensure that your application was received and to let funders know that you are personally invested in the project's success.

SELF-INITIATED FUNDING

Many graphic designers have found innovative ways to generate funding themselves, using the proceeds from the sales of their own designs to fund a cause or charity. In a sense, these designers create microeconomies where their designs become the supply that generates demand. One such example is Drew Marshall, of WorkByDrew, who wanted to support Amnesty International while showcasing local artists in Portland, Oregon. He created a series of coloring books called The Portland Funbook that featured the work of seventy artists. The books were sold at local retailers for five dollars each, of which one dollar was donated to Amnesty International; retailers made two dollars from the sale of each copy, and the remaining two dollars paid for the book's production. All of the five thousand copies Marshall had printed were sold except for a few dozen. The designer was able to donate five thousand dollars to Amnesty International, while at the same time fulfilling his "self-indulgent publishing dreams," as he puts it.[7]

To recommends the tried and true method of selling T-shirts: "A well-designed T-shirt can raise a significant amount of money. We raised over ten thousand dollars for our Well-Done campaign, which is helping to build wells in Africa."[8] BRUTE LABS raised this money with the support of local partners and an impressive online campaign, but this approach can be scaled back to meet or offset the funding needs of smaller design projects.

Charles Nix, a board member of the Type Design Club, uses the New York City Marathon each year as an opportunity to raise money for college scholarships. His online campaign 26 Letters for 26 Miles is based on his love of typography: The designer sells letters of the alphabet to "typographically minded participants" in exchange for running the marathon. "The format is simple," Nix explains, "buy a letter and your name appears on the web attached to that letter." He designed a beautiful chart that features five variations of each letter and is updated daily with the names of new donors.[9] Nix started the project in 2007 to raise money for Team for Kids, an organization that aims to "provide free or low-cost school and community-based health and fitness programs to children who would otherwise have no access to regular physical activity."[10] In subsequent years, 26 Letters for 26 Miles has raised money for the Type Directors Club scholarship fund, which has been awarding money to promising graphic design students throughout the world since 1994. Over the course of five months in 2009, Nix received 4,614.55 dollars in donations, all of which went to support the Type Design Club scholarships.

The designer initially took inspiration from the Million Dollar Home Page, a website that the British business student Alex Tew created in the summer of 2005 to pay for his education.[11] Tew succeeded in raising one million dollars by selling the use of pixels on his homepage for one dollar each. Companies could buy pixels in increments of one hundred pixels and use the web space to feature their logo, which then linked to their website.

Apart from using your design skills to raise money, you can also utilize one of many powerful crowdfunding websites to solicit funds from individuals throughout the world. Crowdfunding websites, such as Kickstarter, RocketHub, and IndieGoGo, have helped tens of thousands of groups and individuals raise millions of dollars for a variety of projects. Brian Meece, RocketHub cofounder and CEO, explains the concept of these sites: "In ages past, wealthy patrons would commission works of art such as symphonies from the recognizable artists and musicians of the day. Crowdfunding is the same idea, but rather than looking for a large contribution from a wealthy patron, artists and entrepreneurs (creatives) look for small contributions from lots of people."[12]

While the various crowdfunding websites target a range of industries, they all provide a similar interface for people to create, share, fund, and manage their projects, and take only a small percentage of the money raised.

COMMUNITY-SUPPORTED MICROGRANTS

While many of us have become comfortable with the process of donating to a project, cause, or charity online, a new grassroots movement has been countering this trend: Community-supported microgrants are the result of groups of dedicated locals meeting in person and collectively deciding how much money to grant projects. The idea for these so-called microgrants gained steam with Sunday Soup in Chicago and has spread to more than thirty cities in the United States, and even a few in Europe. Abigail Satinsky, Sunday Soup cofounder and organizer, described the origins of the program in *Proximity Magazine* 7: "We took inspiration from Saturday Soup, a weekly soup delivery service project in Grand Rapids, Michigan, along with other cottage industry initiatives where enterprising people connect with their neighborhood and make a little money on the side."[13]

In all variations of this event, local community members pay an affordable price to share a meal, while listening to proposals for small to medium-sized art and community-based projects. At the end of the presentation participants vote on how to distribute the profits from the meal to one or all of the proposals. As the Sunday Soup website describes: "With Soup, community participation in the grant funding and selection process is key. Applying for a grant is intentionally simple and unbureaucratic in order to encourage broad participation. This enables us to stimulate and promote experimental, critical, and imaginative practices that may not be eligible for formal funding. While the Sunday Soup grant raises money, it also serves as a way to build a network of support and community that reaches beyond purely monetary assistance. We like to think of it as an open platform to discuss ongoing projects with new audiences, meet new collaborators, and share ways of working."[14]

The founders of FEAST (Funding Emerging Art with Sustainable Tactics) were inspired by Sunday Soup's program and adapted the model for New York City.[15] The organization charges patrons twenty dollars for dinner and a chance to vote on projects. The FEAST events occur quarterly and grant between one thousand to fifteen hundred dollars to between one and three projects. From 2009 until the time of writing this book, FEAST has produced ten dinners, featured twenty-four projects and raised over fifteen hundred thousand dollars. "Because it is located in New York City, FEAST leverages a connection to more art worlds, more communities, and more dollars," explains Sarah Sandman on behalf of the over twenty partners who run the organization. "It simply draws a bigger crowd, brings in more applications, and receives more attention" than their counterparts in different parts of the country. It also helps that FEAST found a generous corporate sponsor in Brooklyn Brewery.

Baltimore's version of Sunday Soup, STEW, features "high-end, locally sourced, maximally organic, and expertly prepared food (including a vegan option)," as STEW organizers state. "We share a desire to rethink participatory ways of funding projects we see as relevant and important in our cities."[16] The organization found corporate sponsorship in local farmers and food vendors, who donate all of the food for the events. Guests pay ten dollars for this multicourse dinner, during which they listen to presentations about art and social justice initiatives and vote on funding them. STEW occurs six to twelve times a year and three to six projects are featured during each meal. As many as seventy-two groups and individuals receive between seventy-five and five hundred dollars per event, along with increased exposure and the possibility of material and human support.

Community-based microgrants rely on the ability of their organizers to share the burden of regularly organizing and running these events. As Satinsky explains, "It will become a sustainable model based on the group's level of commitment to making it work." Sunday Soup's organizers provide the following suggestions for others who want to raise money in a similar way:

+ Find a space for people to cook and eat soup. This could be someone's apartment, a public building, or a city park.[18]
+ Schedule guest cooks, purchase supplies, and promote the event.
+ Put out a call for proposals for your soup grant.
+ Send proposal descriptions to each month's soup customers and ask that they vote for one project.
+ Establish a consistent time and place to build an engaged and committed community.
+ Sell the soup for a modest profit.
+ Gather contact information for each customer.
+ Distribute the grant according to the vote.
+ Document your activities and share your experiences with others.
+ Think about other ways you can collectively fundraise.[17]

NONPROFIT DESIGN STUDIOS

Designers who operate a studio may consider setting up a nonprofit branch of their firm in order to fund pro bono projects, similar to the two nonprofit design organizations featured in this book: Firebelly Foundation, started by Firebelly, and Society of Design (SOD), which grew out of Go Welsh. The nonprofit branches of these design studios allow them to work on projects that directly support their local communities. While you can work on such projects without establishing a nonprofit, there are particular advantages to doing so. You can brand a nonprofit to achieve very different goals than your for-profit business. Your nonprofit can be based on a single cause or mission, which, in turn, may attract a different kind of community than your regular studio. One of the greatest benefits of starting a nonprofit is to receive tax breaks that may help your nonprofit succeed. SOD has utilized these advantages and serves as a good example of how a design nonprofit can make a big impact on its community.

Craig Welsh created SOD in 2009 in order to promote multidisciplinary design education, to harness the community's desire for an elevated design discourse in Central Pennsylvania, and to raise money for worthy causes. As Welsh explains, "The design education and events portion of SOD was in large part a reaction to several of my students at Penn State Harrisburg expressing interest in being exposed to more design. The community service/social impact projects portion simply seemed like the right thing to do—attach design to community initiatives." It took Welsh only six week to make his idea a reality. (Numerous books and websites describe the process of setting up a nonprofit. For example, the Society of Nonprofit Organizations, www.snpo.org, has done a good job of thoroughly outlining these steps.[19])

SOD receives the majority of its income from membership fees. The benefits of membership include eligibility to take part in design competitions and exhibitions, and free access to SOD's quarterly speakers series that has included Chip Kidd, Armin Vit, Michael Rock, Steven Heller, and Jake Barton, among others. SOD also organizes design outings for members, such as trips to Frank Lloyd Wright's Falling Water in western Pennsylvania and the Type Directors Club in New York City. In turn, members agree to volunteer at least ten hours of their time when they join SOD.

Other sources of income are ticket sales to non-SOD members and merchandise SOD staff sells at events. The net proceeds of both are given to charities or other nonprofit organizations; SOD keeps only enough to cover operational costs. Welsh's goal is to eventually be able to spend the same amount of money on events, trips, and exhibitions as the organization gives away to charity, an amount of twenty thousand dollars in the first year. SOD's membership has grown to 230 in the past two years, and as its membership increases, so will SOD's ability to give money to other organizations. Welsh credits the nonprofit's stability to the network of other organizations SOD partners with. "There is tremendous power and many advantages in partnering with other nonprofits," he advises. "Don't just talk to the audiences who can help fund things; speak with other people running nonprofits and seek ways to partner."

While SOD uses design events to raise money for charity, your nonprofit can support community members in any number of ways. Firebelly launched Firebelly Foundation to help its neighbors who were struggling to pay for their basic needs. Look around your local community, see what issues are affecting your neighbors, and determine whether starting a nonprofit would help you address the problem.

Endnotes

PREFACE

1. Bernard Canniffe started Design Coalition in 2002 as a collaboration with Johns Hopkins University. Since the fall of 2009, Ryan Clifford has taught this class. http://www.micasocialdesign.com/overview-dc.
2. "Neurofibromatosis," KidsHealth.org, accessed March 25, 2011, http://kidshealth.org/parent/general/aches/nf.html#/.
3. "Human-Centered Design Toolkit," IDEO website, accessed July 2009, http://www.ideo.com/work/human-centered-design-toolkit.
4. "Design for Social Impact: a How-To Guide," IDEO website, accessed October 2009, www.ideo.com/images/uploads/news/pdfs/IDEO_RF_Guide.pdf.
5. "Design Revolution Toolkit," Design Revolution Road Show website, accessed February 2010, http://designrevolutionroadshow.com/toolkit.
6. Kenneth D. Butterfield, Richard Reed, and David J. Lemak, "An Inductive Model of Collaboration from the Stakeholder's Perspective," Business & Society 43, no. 2 (2004): 162–95, doi: 10.1177/0007650304265956.
7. "Community Engagement Strategies: Tip Sheet," Prevention by Design website, accessed May 22, 2006, http://socrates.berkeley.edu/~pbd/pdfs/Community_Engagement_Strategies.pdf.
8. William Drenttel, "Design and Consequence" (presented at A Better World by Design, Providence, Rhode Island, October 2, 2009), http://vimeo.com/11248186.

IMMERSE YOURSELF

1. Aaron Schutz, "Home Is a Prison in the Global City: The Tragic Failure of School-Based Community Engagement Strategies," Review of Educational Research 76, no. 4 (2006): 691–743.

2. James Cavaye, "Governance and Community Engagement: The Australian Experience," in Participatory Governance: Planning, Conflict Mediation and Public Decision-Making in Civil Society, ed. W. Robert Lovan, Michael Murray, and Ron Shaffer (Burlington, VT: Ashgate, 2004), 85–102.
3. "Community Engagement Strategies: Tip Sheet," Prevention by Design website, accessed May 22, 2006, http://socrates.berkeley.edu/~pbd/pdfs/Community_Engagement_Strategies.pdf. The size of a focus group "usually ranges between five to ten people and is coordinated by a facilitator and a note taker who observes the group interaction. Focus groups can be a source of community input that is enhanced by the dialogue among members when asked focused questions."
4. Cornelia Dragne, Background Document for the University of Victoria Task Force on Civic Engagement (Victoria, BC: University of Victoria, 2007).
5. "Community Engagement Strategies: Tip Sheet," Prevention by Design website, accessed May 22, 2006, http://socrates.berkeley.edu/~pbd/pdfs/Community_Engagement_Strategies.pdf.
6. Butterfield, Reed, and Lemak, "An Inductive Model of Collaboration," 162–95.
7. Cavaye, "Governance and Community Engagement," 85–102.

CARES MOBILE SAFTEY CENTER

1. Office of Epidemiology and Planning, Childhood Injury Deaths in Baltimore City, 2002–2006 (Baltimore: Baltimore City Health Department, 2008), http://www.baltimorehealth.org/info/2008_02_07.CFR%20Report.pdf.
2. Kira McGroarty, Eileen McDonald, Stephanie Parsons, and Andrea Gielen, "The CareS Safety Center: A Mobile Injury Prevention Center for Urban Families" (presented at SOPHE 60th Annual Meeting, Philadelphia, PA, November 6, 2009), http://www.sophe.org/Sophe/PDF/2009%20AM%20presentations/IIA-program%20inn/SOPHE_11.06.09.pdf.
3. "CareS Mobile Safety Center Focus of New Ad Campaign," Johns Hopkins Bloomberg School of Public Health website, accessed June 29, 2009, http://www.jhsph.edu/publichealthnews/articles/2009/gielen_injury_ads.html.
4. "Overview," Center for Design Practice website, accessed July 18, 2011, http://danube.mica.edu/cdp
5. "Process," Center for Design Practice website, accessed July 18, 2011, http://danube.mica.edu/cdp.
6. Tim Parsons, "Johns Hopkins CareS Mobile Safety Center Hits the Streets," JHU Gazette, August 16, 2004, http://www.jhu.edu/~gazette/2004/16aug04/16cares.html.

GREEN PATRIOT POSTERS

1. "Canary Project—About," Canary Project website, accessed October 9, 2011, http://canary-project.org/about-us.

BUILD TRUST

1. "Community Engagement Strategies: Tip Sheet," Prevention by Design website, accessed May 22, 2006, http://socrates.

berkeley.edu/~pbd/pdfs/Community_Engagement_
Strategies.pdf.

2. Butterfield, Reed, and Lemak, "An Inductive Model of
Collaboration," 162–95.

3. "Design for Social Impact Workbook and Toolkit for the
Rockefeller Foundation: Manifesting a Call to Action," IDEO
website, accessed July 2009, http://www.ideo.com/work/
design-for-social-impact-workbook-and-toolkit.

A BOOK BY ITS COVER

1. Charles E. Hurst, *Social Inequality: Forms, Causes, and
Consequences* (Boston: Pearson Education, 2007).

PROMISE ONLY WHAT YOU CAN DELIVER

1. Cavaye, "Governance and Community Engagement," 85–102.

2. "Design for Social Impact: a How-To Guide," IDEO website,
accessed October 2009, www.ideo.com/images/uploads/
news/pdfs/IDEO_RF_Guide.pdf.

MADE IN MIDTOWN

1. New York City Economic Development Corporation,
Strengthening NYC's Fashion Wholesale Market (New
York: Office of the Mayor, 2009), http://nycfashioninfo.com/
getdoc/8dc193de-9b7d-48fc-9d45-edf9aada3379/NYC-
Fashion-Wholesale-Report_081209.aspx.

2. Ibid.

3. Adrienne Pasquarelli, "Garment Center Rezoning Shelved,"
Crain's New York Business, June 14–20, 2010.

PROJECTOPEN

1. "LAHSA—Homelessness Data & Demographics," Los
Angeles Homeless Services Authority website, accessed
August 30, 2011, http://www.lahsa.org/homelessness_data/
reports.asp.

CONFRONT CONTROVERSY

1. Cynthia Hardy and Nelson Phillips, "Strategies of
Engagement: Lessons from the Critical Examination
of Collaboration and Conflict in an Interorganizational
Domain," Organization Science 9, no. 2 (1998): 217–30.

2. "How Can We Communicate Best?" The Designers Accord
website, accessed February 18, 2011, http://edutoolkit.
designersaccord.org/how-can-we-communicate-best.

THE IMPORTANCE OF DIALOGUE

1. "Payday Lending—Policy and Legislation," Center for
Responsible Lending website, accessed September 11, 2011,
http://www.responsiblelending.org/payday-lending/policy-
legislation/.

2. "FDIC Supervisory Policy on Predatory Lending," Federal
Deposit Insurance Corporation website, January 22, 2007,
http://www.fdic.gov/news/news/financial/2007/fil07006.html.

STORIES OF THE CITY

1. "Ground-Breaking Study of Video Viewing Finds Younger
Boomers Consume More Video Media than Any Other Group,"

Council for Research Excellence website, accessed
July 18, 2011, http://www.researchexcellence.com/
news/032609_vcm.php.

2. "Time Spent at Work, at Play and Asleep," WSJ.com,
May 4, 2009, http://online.wsj.com/public/resources/
documents/st_oecd_20090504.html.

IDENTIFY THE COMMUNITY'S STRENGTHS

1. "Community Engagement Strategies: Tip Sheet,"
Prevention by Design website, accessed May 22, 2006,
http://socrates.berkeley.edu/~pbd/pdfs/Community_
Engagement_Strategies.pdf.

2. Cornelia Dragne, Background Document for the University
of Victoria Task Force on Civic Engagement (Victoria, BC:
University of Victoria, 2007), 16. City University's strategic
plan: "Community engagement is made effective through
the development of social capital, that is the extent and
quality of citizen's social engagement with the life of
their communities. Social capital provides citizens with
the information, the social networks and the personal
confidence to engage with the world around them in a
productive way."

REASON TO GIVE

1. "Chicago Wants Feds to Fund Failed Broadband Effort,"
The Heartland Institute website, accessed December 12,
2009, http://www.heartland.org/full/26470/Chicago_
Wants_Feds_to_Fund_Failed_Broadband_Effort.html.

ES TIEMPO

1. F. Altekruse et al., eds., SEER Cancer Statistics Review,
1975–2007 (Bethesda, MD: National Cancer Institute, 2010).

2. "About—Mission," Design Matters at Art Center website,
accessed July 18, 2011, http://www
designmattersatartcenter.org.

UTILIZE COMMUNITY RESOURCES

1. Cavaye, "Governance and Community Engagement,"
85–102. Cavaye states this in the context of the "issues and
challenges" of governmental community engagement in
Australia. His full statement includes, "First, the idea of
'building community capacity' undervalues the existing
often informal capacity of communities and reinforces
paternal approaches to communities. Community capacity
building needs to be reframed into capacity appreciation
or extension, or helping local people build their
community's capacity."

WET WORK

1. "The Reversal of the Chicago River," American Public
Works Association website, accessed July 18, 2011, http://
www2.apwa.net/about/awards/toptencentury/chica.htm.

2. "The Great Lakes' Water: Liquid Gold," The Economist
online, May 20, 2010, http://www.economist.com/
node/16167886.

3. "Moving Design Inspires and Elevates the Culture of Communication around Our Most Pressing Social and Environmental Issues," Moving Designs website, accessed June 12, 2011, http://www.movingdesign.com/experience/about.
4. "Infrastructures for Change Symposium 2010: Great Lakes Models," Infrastructures for Change website, accessed July 19, 2011, http://www.archeworks.org/workshop/index.html.
5. "A Love Letter For You," A Love Letter for You website, accessed July 18, 2011, http://www.aloveletterforyou.com.
6. Moving Design, *Moving Design, Call to Action: A Moving Design Initiative on Water* (San Francisco: Blurb, 2011), http://www.blurb.com/bookstore/detail/1980814.

DESIGN WITH THE COMMUNITY'S VOICE

1. Cavaye, "Governance and Community Engagement," 85–102.
2. Jeremy Lehrer, "Giving Voice," Design 21—Social Design Network website, accessed July 18, 2011, http://www.design21sdn.com/feature/2500.
3. "Design Revolution Toolkit," Design Revolution Road Show website, accessed February 2010, http://designrevolutionroadshow.com/toolkit/.

VENDOR POWER!

1. "Puschart Wars," *Gotham Gazette*, March 22, 2004, http://www.gothamgazette.com/article/iotw/20040322/200/923.
2. Candy Chang, "Making Policy Public: Vendor Power!" Urban Omnibus website, May 6, 2009, http://urbanomnibus.net/2009/05/making-policy-public-vendor-power/.
3. Ibid.
4. Ibid.
5. Ibid.
6. Ibid.

THE 1% USER MANUAL

1. "Quick Facts About Nonprofits," National Center for Charitable Statistics (NCCS) website, accessed July 18, 2011, http://nccs.urban.org/statistics/quickfacts.cfm.

GIVE COMMUNITIES OWNERSHIP

1. Cavaye, "Governance and Community Engagement," 85–102.

PECANS!

1. "Greensboro, Alabama Census Data & Community Profile," AmericanTowns.com, http://www.americantowns.com/al/greensboro-information.
2. Auburn University's Rural Studio, for example, has been located in Hale County since 1993.
3. "About The Program," Design Ignites Change website, accessed July 18, 2011, http://www.designigniteschange.org/pages/2-about.

4. "Labeling & Nutrition: Food Labeling and Nutrition Overview," FDA website, last updated March 23, 2011, http://www.fda.gov/food/labelingnutrition/default.htm.

HAWTHORNE COMMUNITY CENTER

1. "Hawthorne Center," Design Think website, accessed July 18, 2011, http://cargocollective.com/designthink#555040/ H-A-W-T-H-O-R-N-E-C-E-N-T-E-R.

FUNDING SOCIAL DESIGN

1. "Design for Social Impact: a How-To Guide," IDEO website, accessed July 2009, www.ideo.com/images/uploads/news/pdfs/IDEO_RF_Guide.pdf. The toolkit goes on to say: "Our clients value the work more when they pay for it and will dedicate the necessary resources to make it succeed. As a management consulting firm advised, 'Be explicit about who the client is. Watch for scope creep from clients who aren't paying for services.'"
2. "Design Donation," Zerofee website, accessed May 30, 2011, http://www.zerofee.org.
3. Melissa Tioleco-Cheng, email message to author, May 30, 2011.
4. Christine Gaspar, email message to author, March 17, 2011.
5. Craig Welsh, email message to author, March 26, 2011.
6. Ramzy Masri, email message to author, March 14, 2011.
7. Drew Marshall, email message to author, August 20, 2010.
8. Josh To, phone conversation with author, March 8, 2011.
9. "26 Letters for 26 Miles," Sponsor Charles Nix and Support Design Education, accessed March 15, 2011, http://www.charlesnix.com/#map.
10. "Team for Kids," accessed April 29, 2011, http://www.nyrrf.org/get_involved/team_for_kids/about.asp.
11. "Million Dollar Homepage—Own a Piece of History," Million Dollar Homepage, accessed April 29, 2011, http://www.milliondollarhomepage.com.
12. Brian Meece, email message to the author, March 13, 2011.
13. Abigail Satinsky, "How to Grow," Proximity Magazine, accessed March 15, 2011, http://proximitymagazine.com/2010/06/how-to-grow.
14. Abigail Satinsky, "How To Grow," Sunday Soup website, accessed March 12, 2011, http://www.sundaysoup.org/resource/how-grow.
15. Sarah Sandman (on behalf of FEAST), email message to author, April 24, 2011.
16. Nicolas Wisniewski (on behalf of STEW), email message to author, March 16, 2011.
17. "Soup is not an essential element, it is just a cheap and easy way to get started," Sunday Soup website, accessed March 12, 2011, http://sundaysoup.org/soup-network.
18. "The Soup Network," Sunday Soup website, accessed March 12, 2011, http://sundaysoup.org/soup-network.
19. "Starting Up a Nonprofit," Society of Nonprofit Organizations website, accessed on July 4, 2011, http://www.snpo.org/resources/startup.php.

Index